There's Always Something Going Right:

Workbook for Implementing the Nurtured Heart Approach in School Settings

Tammy F. Small, M.Ed.
and
Louisa Triandis, LCSW

There's Always Something Going Right:
Workbook for Implementing the Nurtured Heart Approach in School Settings
Copyright 2010 by Tammy F. Small, M.Ed.
and Louisa Triandis, LCSW

For information contact:
NurturedHeart.net
7132 134th CT SE
Newcastle, WA 98059
tammyfsmall@gmail.com
www.nurturedheart.net
ltriandis@nurturedheartconsulting.com
www.nurturedheartconsulting.com

Cover photography provided with permission by iStockphoto, Cover design by Stephen Huson; Book design by James Giolitto; Copy editing by Dena Klingler, Harry Triandis and Pola Triandis

Printed by Createspace.com

Library of Congress Card Catalog Number: Pending

ISBN 978-0-615-33259-8

Printed in the United States
First Printing: January 2010

Louisa Triandis, LCSW, CNHT

Louisa is a Licensed Clinical Social Worker (LCSW) with over 15 years of counseling experience with families, adults and children of all ages. She is currently an adjunct professor for the University of Southern California School of Social Work. Louisa is also a certificated school social worker and has worked in settings for severely emotionally disturbed children (as well as regular education) supporting teachers with classroom management since 1994. She is a Certified Nurtured Heart Approach trainer, and holds a certificate in art therapy. She provides counseling, coaching and training in both English and Spanish. Louisa received her B.S. from Northwestern University and her Master of Social Work from The University of Illinois. She lives near San Diego with her husband, Jim, and two boundless energy boys, Alex and Nico.

Tammy Small, M.Ed.

An educator for over 27 years, Tammy has worked at all grade levels as teacher, coach, and school counselor. Currently, she thrives as the counselor and NHA coach in a K-8 school where she teaches daily and coordinates a Golden Apple winning Peer Mediation program. Tammy trains schools across the state and speaks nationally to educators and parents on implementing the Nurtured Heart Approach (www.nurturedheart.net). She holds her B.A. from Western Washington University (1984) where she was nominated Outstanding Elementary School graduate, her Masters from the University of Washington in 1995, as well as a Writer's Certificate (2000) and a Certificate in Child and Adolescent Mental Health (2005) from the same university. Tammy lives near Seattle, is a mom of two vibrantly dynamic teenage girls, Maddison and Braeden – and one mellow Wheaten Terrier, Bear.

ACKNOWLEDGEMENTS:

Tammy and Louisa would like to first honor Howard Glasser, creator of the Nurtured Heart Approach. Through his generous mission to bring this system of relationship to all schools and families, he has supported the creation of our workbook and independent trainings across the country. Additionally, Tom Grove, co-author of *The Inner Wealth Initiative* has allowed us to borrow and adapt fantastic activities and creative tools to bring the book's intention to life. Lisa Bravo and Gabrielli LaChiara, two other advanced trainers working with Howie and Tom, were key in infusing the Nurtured Heart Approach into our own passions and lifestyles. Both talented and gifted therapists and trainers, Lisa (with her direct approach) and Gabi (with her compassionate understanding), have been instrumental – and inspirational to both of us. We have also been incredibly inspired and supported by the live-action NHA results of Dr. Susan Zola, middle school principal and dear friend. All of these mentors have demonstrated to Louisa and Tammy what it is to live fearlessly in your Greatness every day.

We also owe great gratitude to friends and family who supported our intentions and also shared their own talents and resources. To Catherine and Albert for sharing their home with us to meet and write, Steve (Tammy's fiancé) for feeding and taking care of us (always) and for his persistence with font and photo dilemmas, Jim (Louisa's husband) for holding down the fort when Louisa took time to write and handling various computer crises (in the most nurturing way), our parents for endless editing and re-editing, and most significantly, our children. Through this work we have learned by example how to be fearless in energizing Qualities of Greatness in our children and their capacity to follow rules. We are honored to be both challenged (and delightfully empowered) by the energy of young boys (Alex and Nico) and the humor and intention of teenage girls (Maddison and Braeden). We are also so blessed to be on this journey with each other.

There's Always Something Going Right:
Workbook for Implementing the Nurtured Heart Approach in School Settings

By: Tammy F. Small, M.Ed. and Louisa Triandis, LCSW

Copyright 2010

Table of Contents

Chapter 1:   1

A REFRESHER OF THE NURTURED HEART APPROACH: Triandis/Small Adaptations from the Trenches

     Empty Praise versus NHA Recognition

     The Three Core Constructs of NHA

     Start Small: How to Train Rover

     Camera, Scrapbooks, Maps and Decoys: Tools for Recognition

     Consequences Nurtured Heart Style

Chapter 2:   14

WHAT'S DIFFERENT IN A NURTURED HEART SCHOOL: School Climate the NHA Way

     Is our building ready to go Nurtured Heart?

     Evaluating Your Building's Progress in Implementing NHA

Chapter 3:   20

WHY IS IT SO HARD SOMETIMES? Challenges to Implementing the Nurtured Heart Approach in your Classroom

     Setting Up The NHA Classroom

     Introducing and Using Resets/Time-outs

     An Extra Dose of Adult Relationship: Secret Mentors

Chapter 4:   **31**

UPHOLDING THE 3-LEGS OF YOUR CLASSROOM: Exercises for Making NHA Your Own

    Exercise #1: Teacher Questionnaire

    Exercise #2: HOW WOULD YOU HANDLE THIS?

    Exercise #3: Try This!

    Exercise #4: Tracking Your Ratio of Positive, Neutral and Negative Comments

    Cheat Sheet for Exercise #2

    SKILLS OF A STUDENT: Group Activity and directions

Chapter 5:   **53**

HOW THE NURTURED HEART APPROACH CHANGES THE ROLE OF THE SCHOOL COUNSELOR

    Helping Kids Name Their Q.O.G.s

    Academic/Behavioral Conversations in the Counseling Office

    Counselor NHA Questions for Consideration or Conversation

Chapter 6:   **65**

HOW DISCIPLINE LOOKS DIFFERENT IN THE NURTURED HEART SCHOOL: Using Buddy Rooms as a Support Tool

    In-School Success (versus Suspension)

    How to use the Discipline Forms

    Let's Get Back on Track!

    Opportunity for Restorative Justice: *Teacher/Student Form*

    Reparation Form – Student

    Parent Letter for Student Suspension

    School Peace Treaty

    A Sample of a Nurtured Heart Discipline Plan

Chapter 7:   92

INFUSING THE NURTURED HEART APPROACH INTO THE FACULTY
CLIMATE

    The Nurtured Heart Moment

    The Dilemma Discussion Moment

    Bringing Classified Staff on Board with NHA

    Supplemental Reading Activities

    Visual Reminders

    Book Discussion and Reflection Questions

    The Power of Our Voice: Group Activities and Directions

    How Administrators and Coaches Can Support Teachers in the Classroom

Chapter 8:   108

USING THE NURTURED HEART APPROACH IN PARENT/ TEACHER/
STUDENT MEETINGS

    Student Success Meeting Form

Chapter 9:   113

WHAT ABOUT THE PLAYGROUND? Simple Tips for Bringing NHA to Other
Schoolhouse Settings

    Some ideas for Playground Staff

    Lunchroom – Kids 2nd favorite place

    The Bus: Ride to Greatness

Chapter 10:   118

RUNNING CLASS MEETINGS: Bringing out the Best Version of Your Classroom

    Establishing the Routine

    Tools for Discussion/Curriculum

    Energizing the Greatness

Chapter 11: 123

BYSTANDER EMPOWERED: Using NHA to Address Peer Relationships and Bullying

Questions for Engaging Bystanders:

Intentional Questions

Intentional Questions: Connecting Students to a Bigger Picture

Chapter 12: 140

SHIFTING THE ENERGY IN A PEER MEDIATOR PROGRAM FROM THE STUDENT PROBLEM TO THE STUDENT STRENGTH: Tammy's take on NHA and Mediation

Selecting Mediators

Training the Mediators

The Mediation Steps

Forms for Mediation

Chapter 13: 150

BRINGING NHA TO SPECIAL SCHOOL SETTINGS: Group Homes and Day Treatment Centers

Credit System: Ways to Earn Points

Credit System: Ways to Spend Points

Chapter 14: 157

BEFORE YOU CAN NURTURE OTHERS, YOU GOTTA START WITH YOURSELF: Recognizing Greatness

Nurtured Heart Approach Book References 161

A REFRESHER OF THE NURTURED HEART APPROACH:
Triandis/Small Adaptations from the Trenches

The Nurtured Heart Approach (NHA) is a system of relationship where all energy and attention is directed to what is going right, and little or no energy is given toward negative behaviors or choices. Rules are clear. Consequences are swift, emotionless and consistent. Most critically, spirits are renewed quickly back to the best version of each person. Practitioners of this tool, <u>intentionally</u> give verbal energy and recognition to their children, students, others in relationship – and *themselves*, by maintaining focus on the positive.

We all possess qualities of greatness; these core strengths sustain and bring us to success in life and relationships. What NHA demonstrates repeatedly is that the building and naming of these qualities of inner wealth are critical to our ability to demonstrate resilience, to handle mistakes, to recover our innate greatness. It is not our flaws which make us powerful – nor the naming of them. But rather it is our strengths (Qualities of Greatness – Q.O.G.s), which pull us out of mistakes, back to that best version.

Every day, even on the days we make mistakes, we do a lot of things right. And with all the things we do right, we demonstrate greatness. In every day, in ordinary moments there are always examples of ways in which we are being the best we can be. In every day, there are also things that go wrong, where we are not being our best. We can focus on what's good, or we can focus on what's bad.

Where we chose to focus will profoundly affect how we feel about ourselves and others. Think about what you are doing right at this moment. You are reading a workbook. Big deal, right? What if you look a little more closely? You are taking time away from something else you would probably rather do or need to do, because you are hopeful you will learn something useful from this book. You could be doing a lot of other things right now, including deciding right off the bat that this is a waste of your time, but you are sticking with it. What does this say about you as a person? At the very least it says you are such a dedicated professional or parent that you are choosing to make this sacrifice; that you are a motivated learner, open to other ways of looking at people and relationships. If we look at it this way, reading the book IS a big deal!

Other people, especially children, are drawn to this energy. Kids will sometimes go for any kind of attention they can get. Often they figure that the way to get the most adult or peer attention is through negative behavior, and so that's what they will do. As parents and adults working with youth, we may believe we focus our attention on the positive, but in reality we pay the greatest attention when problems arise. If you have ever been to a playground and watched what happens with young kids and their moms, you see great examples of this. The kids are playing; the moms are chatting, and perhaps just watching to make sure that weird man by the drinking fountain is not going to snatch anybody. They really aren't recognizing the myriad of good choices their children are making. Things go fine until one child decides she wants some attention from mom. She will look over to make sure Mom sees her, and then turn around and pop the kid next to her. Suddenly, the moms swing into action. The mom of the offending child runs over and usually does one of two things. She will either yell at the kid (possibly smack her or make her sit out), or she will say something like, "Now love, we have talked about getting along with our friends, and that's not a nice way to treat them. You don't want to hurt your friend, blah, blah, blah..." These words are always said in a very loving way - and with lots of energy.

Similarly, an older child is in class, not wanting to do his work, because it's not nearly as interesting as the other things going on around him. The teacher is at her desk, appreciating the quiet work time, but not giving positive energy to the child for his persistence or work ethic. The child starts messing with his neighbor. The teacher comes over and says in a strained, but encouraging voice, that he needs to leave his neighbor alone. She returns to her seat. The child again begins messing with the neighbor. So the teacher yells. The child keeps on messing with the neighbor, because the attention from the teacher is a LOT more interesting than the work. Pretty soon the teacher gets fed up and sends the child to the principal's office, where he will get to interact with the secretary, whoever else passes through, and finally get some quality one-on-one time with the Big Cheese. Heck, he may even get to visit with the friendly counselor. All of a sudden school, and the relationships engaged by this energy, makes school a lot more interesting to the child.

In each scenario, the child ends up with a very confusing message: If I am doing the right thing; no one notices. If I screw up; people talk to me. Though the child might not like getting yelled at, it is attention nonetheless. It's very easy for children to figure out that they get the most attention when things go wrong, so they make sure to mess up as much as possible. They are rewarded for breaking rules.

The most important piece of NHA is **energy**. When we focus our energy on the things that are going well, that others are doing right, we get more of the good stuff we want to see. People are validated and built up. They are truly *energized* by the experience of having others recognize their greatness. If we put our energy on the negative, we get more of that. Kids want our attention, no matter what. In NHA, we use this intentional energy to build relationship that scaffolds inner wealth.

Empty Praise versus NHA Recognition:
The Difference is in the Intended Result

When we train schools, lead groups or speak to adults who are working toward mastering the Nurtured Heart Approach, we are frequently questioned about the possible "fluffiness" of a system where praise is at the center. The approach is not so much about praise, as it is about what we choose to recognize. We are not just telling people they are great simply to "blow sunshine" their way, but rather, to get them to see the good choices they are making and the ways in which they are already being successful. Recognize that skeptics of heavy positivity take this path. We have all met people who seem to be full of positive "self-regard" but amazingly lack true self -awareness and personal responsibility.

Nurtured Heart recognition focuses on capacity and the specific skills a human being uses to develop character. This recognition is dependent on the irrefutable evidence of the individual's greatness. It is realistic recognition and a focus on the development of core values. We do not tell Susie that she is a strong soccer player or has an amazing voice if these are not true qualities she posses. We <u>do</u> name her capacity to be a strong team player or a dedicated musician. These <u>are</u> true qualities that can be honored. This is the same greatness that allows individuals to learn from mistakes, not <u>focus</u> on them. These are the qualities of resiliency that help an individual bounce back from disappointment and push through a challenge. These are qualities of character that scaffold a person to handle a consequence, to bravely be honest, and to step with maturity and responsibility toward being the kind of leader and team player that we seek in work places, school houses, friendships, marriages, teams, life. The Nurtured Heart recognition differs from praise in the quality and depth, and in the fact that it comes with the expectation that, with Qualities of Greatness, come the ability to follow rules, handle consequences and step up to all that is asked. Nurtured Heart recognition highlights capability of greatness in every situation.

The Three Core Constructs of NHA

Howard Glasser, creator of The Nurtured Heart Approach, refers to the three-legged stool (or table) of NHA. All three legs have to be in place for the approach to work or everything falls apart. When you feel things getting out of control, it is good to think about your stool and figure out what leg has been kicked out. The legs can be summarized as follows:

1) Always fight to find the positive in any moment, and put your energy into it.
2) Refuse to put any energy into anything negative.
3) Always deliver a consequence when things go wrong.

So how do you find the positive? Many times we have gone into a classroom to observe a student and had the teacher say something along the lines of, "Look at Johnny. There he is again causing trouble. He's being disruptive and bothering his neighbor. He hasn't done a bit of work since he came in." This might be true, but it is also true that Johnny is doing some things RIGHT. He might have a paper and pencil out. Maybe he has even written a sentence or two. Maybe at the very moment I am looking at him, he is actually NOT bothering his neighbor! What's going on? Look at the picture below:

Do you see an old woman with a big wart or a young woman with long flowing hair? (Hint if you can't see both: The ear of the young woman is the eye of the old woman. The chin and mouth of the old woman are the neck with a necklace of the young woman.) Both women are there, but it is up to us to decide which woman we want to see. It is the same with all the Johnnys of the world. We can choose to focus on what is beautiful about them or what is ugly and difficult. There is always SOMETHING that a child is doing right, even in his/her most difficult moments. It is up to us to make the decision to find and name that <u>right</u> thing. That may mean lowering the bar and starting with something incredibly basic, like the fact that Johnny is at school. Once we start to show Johnny that he is being successful, and he gets tied into that idea, we can raise the bar. You won't be stuck acknowledging Johnny forever for little things, because Johnny will start to rise to your recognitions.

Start Small: How to Train Rover

Let's use the analogy of training a puppy. Puppies have boundless energy and unconditional love, but also untrained behavior that needs boundaries. Training a puppy is really about consistency, rewards, positive recognition – and positive energy. When a dog is breaking a rule, an owner must be calm but firm, so that the pet learns and is encouraged to follow rules. Additionally, Rover is trained best when you catch him being good – rather than scolding him when he messes up. Even in a cowering position, Rover still begins to learn he gets attention from his owner when he breaks a rule. Start small. Set Rover up for success. Initially, when you call him and he looks up, be effusive with praise. If he steps toward you, do more of the same. Later, only praise when he first steps toward you when called. And then later still, when he comes all the way to your side. And so on.

This shaping of his behavior will require less energy as he gets closer to the goal of "coming when called the first time" and because you 'caught him being good' with a simple move in the right direction, he will move toward that recognition more and more. When house breaking, put him outside and even when he simply sniffs to piddle, praise him. If he begins to piddle inside, say nothing, scoop him up and put him outside. The moment you set him down, praise and pet him; you are wildly excited that he is learning. What does Rover get? All your energy and attention when things are going right! Additionally, you have set him up for getting this attention even in simple, automatic tasks, that will then be shaped by recognition, toward more critical socialization – like coming when called, , not jumping, etc. Set him up for his goodness.

Keep in mind these words of Albert Einstein: "There are only two ways to live your life. One is as though nothing is a miracle. The other is as though everything is a miracle." Watch for the miracles the Johnnys show you, especially when you find yourself feeling frustrated. Even if you feel yourself getting angry, it is essential to keep the negative energy to yourself. *Remember what you are fighting for!* Your ultimate goal is to build a child's inner wealth. A child might start to believe that he really does have the ability to be successful. If you then come and dump negativity all over him for something he has done wrong, you feed into his old image of himself as someone who screws up.

For the parent or teacher, recovering from putting your focus on the negative, or "leaking" can be very hard. The child again has to test whether you are for real. As much as you can, refrain from yelling, rolling your eyes, etc. Also watch out for saying things like "good job, <u>but</u>," or "*so and so* does this so well" (implying that the child being recognized doesn't), etc. [Refer to *The Inner Wealth Initiative*, Chapter 6: Famous Leaks (c.2007) for more in depth explanations of ways we unintentionally give negative energy.] Additionally, help yourself see every child as capable by stepping away from complaining or naming these flaws to your peers or partners. Whatever we name, we <u>see</u>. Whatever we name, we get more of. Name Greatness. See Greatness.

Tom Grove, co-author of *the Inner Wealth Initiative,* once shared with us a core phrase we use often to keep this at the forefront of our goal to nurture capabilities.

> *"There is nothing you can say or do, that will dissuade me from believing in your ability to be successful."*

Camera, Scrapbooks, Maps and Decoys: Tools for Recognition

So how do we focus our energy on the positive and keep from leaking negativity? NHA provides some very useful tools. We want to use all of them to keep the positive energy flowing. The first tool is the Kodak moment, as Howard Glasser originally termed it, or what we like to think of as pulling out your **Camera**. Think of taking a picture of the child, and then describing that picture to someone who can't see it. There is no judgment in the comments about the picture, just a statement of what you see. Here are a couple of examples:

> "I see you sitting at your desk, with your pencil and paper out."
> "You are building a tower of blocks and being really careful to balance them."

These may seem like trivial comments but what they do for a child is make her feel noticed and recognized, just for being present in the world. One advantage of this type of recognition is its simplicity. You name what you see – so people who are somewhat uncomfortable with effusive praise (either receiving or giving) can simply note what is happening. Shining the light on the moment still produces positive regard in the simple, but powerful value of being seen.

Our next tool is the **Scrapbook**; in Glasser's book he refers to these as a Polaroid or active recognition. Think about what you do when you look at a bunch of pictures you have taken. You select the ones that highlight the experience. With the Scrapbook, we label the Qualities of Greatness (Q.O.G.s) within the experience we have captured. This is what we aim to do for the child. We are building a story of his greatness. We pull out the Camera to take a picture, and <u>then</u> explain why that picture is important. This is the tool we use to build up a children's portfolios – and help them own the best version of themselves. These are the "teachable moments," in that they provide us the opportunity to point out to kids the ways in which they have outstanding character. If there is a value you want to see more of, find ways of pointing it out when you see even a little bit of it. Here are a couple of examples:

> "You look angry right now, but you are calm and in control. You have some real anger management skills!"

> "You asked for help in a quiet voice. That was so respectful and polite!"

> "You looked up right away when I asked for your attention. What a powerful listener."

Maps are another powerful tool we use for positive recognition, (cannons or proactive recognition in Glasser's books). We need Maps to negotiate the world and to know where we should and should not go. With NHA, our Maps spell out the rules, and show kids what they need to do to stay on the right road. When we point out all the things they could be choosing to do which would result in a detour from the desired road (i.e. getting a speeding ticket, running out of gas, or getting lost), we give them specific evidence of the positive outcome of their good (but sometimes difficult) choices. This is done NOT as a tool to suggest <u>ways</u> they might detour, but rather as a way of saying, "You're on the right highway." The Maps provide direction and show children where the boundaries are. We should comment on them often to reinforce their choice to follow the rules. Here are some examples:

> "You are in control of your anger right now. You could be yelling, screaming, and swearing at me, you could be throwing things, you could be hitting the walls, but you are in control of your emotions."

> "Wow! I can tell you are frustrated with this assignment, but you are still sticking with it. You didn't give up, put your head down, or tear up your paper."

"You are unhappy, but you are not taking your clothes off and putting them in the toilet!" (This is one of our favorites, since one of our children actually did this at one point!)

Maps are especially helpful when it seems that nothing is going right. There are ALWAYS things that a child could be doing and is NOT doing. When we point these things out, we reinforce how they are aware of the rules and using their power and self-control to stay on the right road. If you make it funny, like the example above, it can help to lighten the mood as well.

Additionally, you should follow each Map statement with a strong Scrapbook statement, which will continue to build the child's positive portfolio. For example:

"This shows a terrific amount of persistence, tenacity, dedication, maturity, willpower, focus, etc..."

Our last tool is **Decoys**, (creative recognition in Glasser's book). We use these to distract a child and pull her into being successful before she realizes what we are doing. We tell her to do something right when she is about to do it anyway, and then nail her with recognition. Here is an example of how this works.

A resistant kid in a class accidentally knocks over a book as he was walking across the room. When he automatically starts bending to pick it up, you say:

"Wow, you knew exactly what I was going to ask you to do. What great insight and cooperation. You picked that up right away!"

Now he might look at you and drop the book on purpose just to see what you will do. BUT chances are, the kid is going to be so stunned by your tactics that he will just put the book down. Then you can start building the Scrapbook.

"You did just what I needed you to do, and are being so helpful."

Have fun with this and be BRAVE! Kids will look at you like you are nuts, but remember what you are after. You are determined to show them their Qualities of Greatness, and the ways in which they are already being successful.

Consequences Nurtured Heart Style

When a child does mess up, we don't want to give warnings or get angry (both forms of leaking negativity), but it is essential that a consequence be given. In the Nurtured Heart Approach, that consequence is always some form of a modified time-out. Glasser and Grove utilized the idea of a computer's reset button as a clear visual of the NHA's intention of a time-out. The term '**reset**' applied to a person is a simple idea of pressing an internal button which essentially 'resets' your internal settings back to your capacity for Greatness. You can use whatever word works best for you and the child. Little kids sometimes like "red light." Older kids like "take a minute" or "center yourself."

Recently, we came up with another way of timing-out a student or child. With so many kids playing team sports, we coined the term, "Sideline." When you are on the sideline of a field, you are NOT IN THE GAME. The goal of all players is to be in the game, so a "sideline" (a simple stop, breath, take-a-minute moment) is requested before they can rejoin. This can be done either in a chair, right on the spot, or in any place in the room standing or sitting. It is essential that this be a brief time-out (10 to 30 seconds seem to work fine for most resets). After the student is calm, handles that consequence and steps to her 'sideline', she is invited back IN THE GAME of life's glorious privileges and rewards (like your attention).

Remember, a reset is NOT a punishment. Many people genuinely struggle with this concept. It is hard for some folks to get over the idea that when kids screw up they have to PAY! The reset simply says, "Oops, you're off the success track, and you need to get back on. Take some time to put yourself back where you need to be." It is really YOU, the adult, removing your attention. Gabrielli LaChiarra, another NHA trainer, talks about "pulling down the shade on negativity." That is really what we are striving to do in a reset and it indicates, "I don't see you right now, so you can't receive my energy." A reset is an opportunity to step back into the best version of ourselves, and a place where all energy is focused toward that goal. The reset always has "the kiss of forgiveness," as Howard says. Practice resetting yourself. Time yourself out when you lose control. Place your hands on your stomach. Take some deep breaths. Tell your student or child you are working with, "I need to reset myself for a second." This makes you an ultimate role model.

As you read the exercises in this book, you will notice these ideas are explored in different settings and reviewed with various examples. As trainers who have worked with hundreds of parents and professionals, we have found that the varied repetition reinforces and instills the concepts so they become the consistent vocabulary for our way of being in <u>every</u> relationship.

WHAT'S DIFFERENT IN A
NURTURED HEART SCHOOL?

Walking into a Nurtured Heart school, you will immediately feel a difference in the school culture from that found in a regular school. Differences are present in every aspect of school life from teachers, to students, to classified staff. While individual building results may vary, schools adopting NHA have generally found a large decrease in their discipline referrals and suspension rates. In one year of dedicated school- wide implementation, schools have achieved as much as a 70 percent decrease in discipline referrals and a 50 percent decrease in number of suspensions. (For many more specific statistics which demonstrate the efficacy of the Nurtured Heart Approach, please visit www.difficultchild.com.)

Deciding to adopt the Nurtured Heart Approach is not easy. Change is always difficult for people, and becoming a true Nurtured Heart school is a process. Schools with high rates of discipline referrals or suspensions are under a great deal of pressure to make changes and may be more receptive to trying something new. On the other hand, it is easy for schools to become complacent if things are "good enough." It is important to ask ourselves as administrators, teachers, counselors, etc., what we can do to make our schools the best they can be, even when they are a "Blue Ribbon School."

Is Our Building Ready to Go Nurtured Heart?

In deciding whether NHA is something the school staff wants to take on, it is helpful for *everyone* on the staff to consider honest answers to some important questions. You can use these questions as a jumping off point for your staff to decide whether it is ready to make the effort to go Nurtured Heart. In italics are the issues to consider when evaluating your school team's answers to each question.

1) Is my school the kind of school where teachers like to work? Why/why not? *Keep an eye out for answers like "No, because our kids are so hard." This is an indication that teachers are feeling as if they don't have the tools to work with their students effectively.*

2) Is my school the kind of school where kids enjoy being? Why/why not? *Watch out for "No, because these kind of kids don't like school."*

3) Do teachers resent staff meetings or look forward to them? *Watch for "Doesn't everyone hate staff meetings?" Meetings do not have to be painful.*

4) How are parents welcomed at school? Is this true for parents of challenging kids? *Watch for differences in how parents are treated.*

5) Is there a clear discipline policy at my school? Do students know the expectations? *Is there a written policy that staff has agreed on? Has this policy also been presented to the students? Everyone should know what the expectations are.*

6) How much bullying occurs? Is our suspension rate as low as it could be? *Any amount is too much, but how does your school compare to others in your district/community? Has your suspension rate been increasing or decreasing?*

7) Are there examples every day of students supporting each other both academically and socially? *Do students tend to compete with each other or cheer each other on?*

8) Do classified staff (aides, playground, lunch room, etc.) feel they are part of the school? What message do they present to students, parents and the community? *Do they seem happy to work at the school? Are they friendly? Do they feel as if they are part of the school team? Do they feel set apart as a different class of staff?*

9) What kind of reputation does my school have in the district and in my community? *If you have a reputation as a tough school, why? If you have a reputation as a good school, what could still be done to strengthen it and maintain growth?*

Evaluating Your Building's Progress in Implementing NHA

If your school has truly gone Nurtured Heart you will see it everywhere. And even if your school has been doing NHA for awhile, keeping the constructs current is critical to consistent results. It can be easy to fall back into old, negative, and more familiar patterns if staff and administrators are not diligent. Here are some things to consider when evaluating your school's progress. Considering these different questions can help indicate the progress you school is making. You can do your own evaluation, but it is more accurate to get input from your whole staff.

1) Walking down the hallways, do you hear teachers using praise and greeting kids warmly? *There should be no yelling at kids about getting to class. Instead, students should hear things like, "Look at Joey navigate that hallway! He knows he has less than a minute left to get to class and he's gonna get there!"*

2) In the classrooms, do positive comments flow all around the room? Are there a few "good jobs" here and there, or are comments made *throughout* the lesson about how kids are being successful? Are there a lot of student

outbursts? Are those that occur handled quickly but quietly? Does everyone know what the classroom expectations are, and are they strictly enforced? Who gets the most attention and for what? Do the difficult students get recognition for things they are doing well? Do the "good kids" get recognition too? At what rate are positive comments made: once every ten minutes, once every five, once every three? What is the rate of positive to negative comments? *In our NH school, we aim for four positives for every one negative recognition (including resets).*

3) Do staff enjoy going to all staff meetings? Do people come away feeling filled-up rather than drained? Is there a sense of tension or camaraderie among staff members? Do you feel like there are a lot of "politics" at your school? *A meeting is still a meeting, but there should be an upbeat feel, and staff should not dread going. The most effective meetings occur when nurturing relationships between the adults is at the core.*

4) A question for parents whose children are suspended or brought in for disciplinary meetings: Do you feel supported and acknowledged for how you have parented your child in relation to school or have you been made to feel like a bad parent? *Parents of spirited children have usually gone through the wringer a number of times. They may really dread meetings or any contact with the school. It is critical to nurture your partnership with them.*

5) What happens when kids make poor choices? Are clear consequences delivered with no fanfare? Are all discussion/lectures saved for after the child has completed the consequence and do they focus on how s/he can be successful? Are there mixed messages students get about the amount of time you get with staff when you mess up? *This last piece can be really hard to avoid and it is essential to get creative about giving needy kids the extra time before problems start, not after. When a child does get into trouble, remember to just deliver the consequence-that's it. No lectures!*

6) How much bullying takes place? *In an NHA school there will be less bullying as kids are more supportive of each other. There will be fewer fights and a reduction of racial tension.*

7) Do students encourage and support each other? *The level of competition between children should be reduced because all are getting their needs met. There will be less one-upmanship. Children will model what they see. If their inner wealth is built up, they will start to do it to each other.*

8) Are all students and staff on the same page about the rules? Are all expectations clear? Is everyone aware of the discipline policy? Do teachers appear to have the same expectations? Are spirited children able to be successful in some classes, but are referred more frequently out of others? *If there is a consistent problem in a classroom, that teacher may feel supported with extra coaching.*

9) Is your suspension rate as low as it can be? When you have to suspend a child, is it productive or just a way to get rid of a kid for a few days? How many repeat offenders do you have? *Nurtured Heart is very effective with students in suspension or other discipline situations. See our section on discipline.*

10) Has your average daily attendance gone up? Do students like coming to school? Has participation in your after-school programs increased? *Consider doing a survey of students like the School Connectedness survey to get a sense of how students feel about the school. Below are links to two surveys:*
http://www.asdk12.org/depts/assess_eval/Evaluation/climate_survey/2009_climate_student_3-4.pdf
http://www.asdk12.org/depts/assess_eval/Evaluation/climate_survey/2009_climate_student_5-12.pdf

11) Have your test scores increased? Do teachers get through all of the curriculum they intend to or do they run out of time? Do they have to develop

more curriculum because they get through lessons faster? *As students remain in class, they will learn more and you can expect test scores to rise.*

12) Questions for classified staff: Do classified staff feel acknowledged for their daily contributions? Do they feel connected to the school? Are they friendly and welcoming? Do they understand and use NHA? *There is a tendency for classified staff to be left out of trainings. It is essential that they participate in NHA trainings as much as possible. Remember, **everyone** in the school must be on board. If students arrive at school and are greeted in a warm, friendly way, they will be much more likely to go on and be motivated to have a successful day. Conversely, if students are yelled at by the cafeteria staff, this can set them up for the beginning of a downer afternoon.*

13) Does the community know what your school is doing? Are your NHA trainings open to the community? Is the school considered an asset, or are you seen as decreasing property values? Reputation is important. Does your reputation reflect your values?

In all of the above areas, there will always be room for improvement. The important thing is to keep moving forward. It will be easy to see improvements in data like test scores, number of suspensions and average daily attendance. Additional data provided by surveys like the *School Connectedness Survey* can be very helpful. Administer the surveys at the beginning and end of the year, see how you grow and then what still needs work. If you have seen a decrease in problems in one area followed by resurgence in another, chances are your 3-legged table is off somewhere. The strongest school cultures focus on the positive, putting no energy into the negative and keeping very strict about the delivery of consequences.

WHY IS IT SO HARD SOMETIMES?
Challenges to Implementing the Nurtured Heart Approach
in Your Classroom

The logic of the Nurtured Heart Approach is unarguable. As educators and parents, and all people in relationship, it speaks to our human nature. Have high expectations. Believe in every person's capabilities. Notice what is right. Ignore what isn't. Create consistent rules. Be strict in upholding them. Sure, makes sense.

So why is it so hard? The reality is that most of us have been raised in the upside down system of attention for negative behavior. We approach this new idea with skepticism and doubt and old habits of relationship. We struggle with our inability to ignore an arguing child. Our compassionate nature wants to say, "Well, next time..." And our nagging conscience can't wrap itself around everyone's need to be recognized – even as we meet the most basic classroom expectation. "Isn't that what they are supposed to do anyway," our Sally Skeptic says. It sounds silly saying, "Way to focus, John!" or "I see this whole back table with eyes on me." "You came in with such purpose and are so ready to work." Ah, but this is where we are called to Greatness. Risk being seen as "silly" – because the payoff is fabulous.

Many people comment that doing Nurtured Heart Approach seems too difficult. Older teachers will remark that their form of classroom management has been working just fine for 20 years, and they have no need to change. The interesting thing is that if these same teachers really give Nurtured Heart a try, they become convinced, because teaching becomes remarkably easier. A veteran teacher Louisa worked with decided to take on Nurtured Heart as part of her professional development goals. She was very "old school" in her approach to discipline. She kept a journal of her experiences using the approach over the course of the school year. At the end of the year she wrote that she was "looking forward to next year's challenges" and that "to feel that way in May was exciting!" In previous years, by the time May rolled around she was burnt out and counting the days. With Nurtured Heart she "could have gone another three months!"

The other challenge to Nurtured Heart is that it goes against what we have always known. It is difficult to unlearn old habits of yelling or sending students out of the classroom for misbehavior. We encourage new teachers that Nurtured Heart will be easy for them because they don't have to unlearn anything, but for veteran teachers old habits can die hard. It is helpful to have a teacher buddy, who will consult with you and even watch your class, if possible, to help remind you to keep your three legs strong.

There are few arguments that will not collapse under the transforming quality of your Relentless Pursuit of the Positive. And the funny thing about this is that EVERYONE WANTS TO BE SEEN. There is a reason a child brags or a bully teases. Attention is sought - energy is given (even in socially inappropriate ways) because everyone craves it.

When Tammy first began using the Nurtured Heart Approach as a teacher and counselor, she recalls one of her 8th grade students commenting after several lessons: "Mrs. Small, did you just get back from some class or motivational workshop or something?" Here was a boy who lacked impulse control and previously received a lot of attention for his negative acting-out behavior.

"Why, Gary?"

He shrugged, "Well, you seem to be complimenting everyone and telling everyone what you like and being all positive and stuff. Like more than usual."

"Hmmm... well, does that bother you?"

He was quiet for a minute (that in itself, a quality worth energizing), and then smiled broadly, "No, I kinda like it."

It was pure, genuine joy and you can bet she energized the question, the risk, the engagement, the inquisitive nature of his personality. His insight.

While it is our intention to always see what is going right, the real challenge many face is to keep focus there – and not be drawn toward energizing the negative (i.e. when Gary does talk out of turn, when Gary distracts his neighbor, when Gary gets out of his seat without permission, etc.). Our authentic goal is to name the students around Gary who are following directions, to give a quick, energy-less reset to Gary when he breaks a rule, to then quickly welcome Gary back and recognize the maturity with which he handled it.

For our frequent resetters (those who have spent most of the years of their lives gaining attention for their negative behaviors), we often have a private conversation separated from the class. Here we name their greatest qualities. We highlight in the conversation how, even in that moment, they are demonstrating such great respect, self-control and wisdom. We call them to honor their greatness – and promise to recognize it frequently. Finally we call on their capabilities – to cooperate, to handle resets, to participate within the rules. The key is to acknowledge the successes they are already demonstrating.

In this chapter on classroom issues, some of these challenges are further explored. The seeming roadblock we run into in implementing the Nurtured Heart Approach so often is connected to our own leaking, our self-criticism, or the habit of a lens which wants to shift toward what isn't working.

As you explain a reset/time-out/take-a-minute to a child or a class, be very clear about your intentions. "Whoops, forgot how great you are" should be the message. You slipped from your Greatness Pedestal. It is not punishment – it is simply a reminder, a nudge back up to the pedestal, quick and without energy, so that the child can rapidly return to the place of glorious Time-In (your classroom).

In this same vein of honorable intention and non-leaking tone you may ask a child to move a seat, take a distraction from their hand, or step away from an activity. "Whoops. Forgot how great you are." Again, explain to the whole class, or the energy-challenged student, that these rewards are theirs to have – the book after class, the toy back after school, rejoining the group and trying again later. "Shoot, Broke a rule. Let's try again tomorrow." And as quickly as you can, recognize how gracious they are in handling the consequence. So capable – and therefore, ready to try again soon (next period, in ten minutes, when they feel they can return to the group, etc.).

What is critically different is YOUR response to the broken rule. Stop the lectures. They know. Stop the warnings and "next times," because the child can handle the consequence the first time. Stop the referrals (unless a school guideline of safety is broken), and give no energy to the rule at all. The real challenge for educators (parents, co-workers, counselors, etc.) is to stop taking broken rules personally. Know that your students want to be seen – and decide to see them as GREAT.

There will be skeptics who staunchly resist your attempts to recognize their Q.O.G.'s (Qualities of Greatness). They want to believe in their own greatness, but have invested much time and energy on pushing others away and garnering attention only from their misbehavior. Stand firm with your message. Be prepared to confront them with their irrefutable power. It is not a matter of whether they can or can't demonstrate greatness, they ARE right now. "Sorry. I think you are great. Here is what I think. So you are stuck with this: Your Greatness. Get over it."

Setting Up the NHA Classroom

The many differences between a regular and a NHA classroom all stem from our intentional shift in focus. In a non-NHA classroom, the teacher generally speaks to students when they need prompting to get on-task. Very little is said when students are doing things right. In a non-NHA classroom, the rules are posted, and when kids break a rule, there is some form of attention and recognition for this. For example, younger children often have the card system, where they are either on green, yellow or red, and they have to change their card color when they make a mistake. Older students often see their names put on the board, with check marks beside them indicating some consequence. When a student misbehaves, he may watch the teacher call his parents in front of the class. This is usually preceded by the threat of the phone call: "Do I need to call your mom about this?"

With Nurtured Heart, this system gets turned upside down. Instead of names on the board for bad behavior, names get put on the board for good behavior. Groups sitting together can earn tally marks for their accomplishments (which should get verbal praise as well). Phone calls home are made for students doing things they should be proud of. They are preceded by "You are working so hard today, I think we are going to need to call your mom half way through class to tell her about it!" Of course, students are recognized for their success, and not for their screw-ups. Whatever we name we get more of; in an NHA classroom, we name success!

You can start to do NHA in your class at any time (even toward the end of the year), and you will get results. Just focusing on the positive will cause things to shift. If you are already into the school year, it is interesting to do experiments to see how your students react and how powerful your energy can be. You might start with the goal of having 80 percent of your comments/interactions be positive and only 20 percent negative (**including resets**). (See the exercises at the end of this chapter.) Remember, you are striving to put as much emphasis on the positive as possible.

When you start to build your students' inner wealth, you will have far fewer discipline issues, but there will still be some behavioral problems that you will need to consequence. You want to make sure students know exactly what is expected of them and what the rules are. Most teachers seem to like to post rules in their classroom, although this is not necessary. (Pre-school kids can't read, but they figure out the rules quickly enough.) If you are going to do so, there is less room for debate if the rules are posted in the negative. For example, "No put - downs" is pretty straightforward. Everyone knows when a put-down has occurred, since nearly anyone who overhears the comment generally reacts. "Be Kind to Others" however, is a lot more nebulous. What does it really mean to "Be Kind"? Your definition may be very different from a child's. When the rules are clear, it is much easier to give a consequence. You know that the child knows what the rules are, so there is no second-guessing yourself and no need to review them when one is broken.

Introducing and Using Resets/Time-outs

There are a couple of ways to introduce the idea of "resets." Remember that we want to start with the first leg of the stool, focusing on the positive. If you are taking time to do that, you will notice kids naturally resetting themselves. Use this opportunity for a Scrapbook statement (one of our recognition tools explained in Chapter one: NHA Refresher). You can say things like:

> "Wow, you walked away from the friend you were having a problem with and reset yourself beautifully."
> "You caught yourself when you were speaking without raising your hand and zipped your mouth. Great reset!"

"Fantastic reset, table four. Way to refocus back into the whole class discussion."

Kids often reset themselves. They catch themselves just before they are heading to break a rule or they apologize for a mistake. Here you can comment on their ability to reset themselves and how powerful that is. Set students up to understand how resets help us get back on track when we get off and how sometimes we have to reset ourselves to keep going in the right direction. Then, when a rule gets broken you can just say, "Oops, broke a rule. Reset yourself." (Or "take a minute", "that's a time out", "red light", etc.). Kids will know what to do, because you have already demonstrated and clarified the concept.

Alternatively, resets can be introduced as an actual lesson in class. Explain that the purpose is just to get students back on track, and that we ALL need to reset ourselves at times. You can talk about a computer resetting when it runs into a problem. Having to reset does not mean you are bad, just that you are going in the wrong direction, and now you need to get going the right way. You can demonstrate how you would like kids to reset themselves so that they can get back in the game as soon as possible. As focused educators, we can often miss a chance to keep a reset brief. Tell older students to welcome themselves back to time-in when they can demonstrate that they are reset (generally less than one minute). Having kids push away from their desks and/or put their heads down is helpful, because it alerts you visually to the fact that they are in a reset and need to be called back. Be sure to explain the welcome back part of the reset, so you show that it really does not have to be a big deal, and is actually just another opportunity to get attention when you do it right. You might say something like:

"I know you all know how to reset, because you have been showing me by correcting yourselves in front of me countless times in the last couple of days! If you get off track, I'll ask you to reset. If you put your head on your desk, I won't forget that you have done what I asked, and I'll be able to welcome you back much more quickly."

Deciding which word to use for reset is important because it needs to be meaningful, and not irritating to kids. We find that younger children sometimes get silly with the word reset, because they actually start to jump around and shake as though they were physically resetting. For younger kids "time-out" can work or "red light." Older students may not like the word reset. Other suggestions are "center yourself," "refocus," "take a minute," or "sideline." You have to be comfortable and consistent with the word you decide to use.

In every class, there is at least one particularly challenging child. These children act out, demonstrate apathy, or simply refuse to do work. They are out of sync with their greatness, and they need an organized attack of inner wealth building. As soon as they enter the room, be sure to connect with them and then keep the connections coming non-stop. You really need to make a concerted effort to nail them at least every five minutes or so with a specific Q.O.G.! Be prepared for them to react badly at first, as they try to figure out if you are for real. Oppositional children are so used to getting their needs met through acting out, it will take some time for them to adjust. Just keep at it. Remember, there is ALWAYS something going right. It is up to you to figure out what that is and what you can say about it. It may take months, but eventually, even the most difficult child will start to turn around.

It helps to get all children, but particularly our spirited children, moving to stay out of trouble. Having them hand out papers is an easy way to let them get out of their seats and move around. Perhaps another leadership position in your classroom provides the same opportunity. Evidence suggests that exercise can help us focus and reduce anxiety. If you have an "ants-in-the-pants" kid, set up an option for her to go outside the class and do ten jumping jacks or run in place for one minute every 15 minutes or so. Praise her for this ability to know what she needs and to regulate herself.

You can also get kids moving without calling attention to them by establishing special systems between teachers. A teacher can write a note and ask a student to take it to another teacher. That teacher signs off on the note and honors the child. The child returns to class, having received attention as well as a chance to move. Teachers can use this opportunity to give a shot of inner wealth to their colleagues by putting some thoughtful words into the notes they send.

Getting the whole class up and moving is helpful for everyone. Whenever you have a transition from one activity to another, think about putting up-beat music on and encouraging people to move a bit. Another good option is to make everyone stand up and do two minutes of exercises halfway through class. Include an exercise where you cross the mid-line of your body. (Your right hand goes across your body to touch your left leg and your left hand touches your right leg). (Check out www.braingym.com for books and resources about exercise to help kids focus in school) Exercise helps wake up the brain and will make everyone more focused and alert. Your ADHD kids will get what they need without having to be singled-out, but everyone (including you), will benefit.

The other type of student that really frustrates teachers is the child who shows up to school, but does absolutely nothing. We cannot count the number of children we have worked with who had this issue and turned out to have an unidentified learning disability, even in high school! Find a moment to ask the child away from other students if he is unable to do the work, or if he is just not interested in it. If you suspect learning disabilities, help facilitate the process for individualized assessment. If there are no learning disabilities, you may be dealing with an issue of depression, which can be debilitating enough to make someone unable to do anything. The fact that the child is showing up at all may be taking all of his/her energy.

Don't fuss at these children to sit up and get to work. Start with acknowledging them for being at school:

> "It's so hard to get up to come to school, and here you are! I recognize that you are using a lot of effort and it's great to have you here."

If they have backpacks, acknowledge their organization:

> "You are at school and you are prepared. You have to be really organized to remember what you need to bring to school."

If they take their pencils out:

> "You have a pencil and you are ready to write!"

Every small step should be honored. Again, think about Rover and recognizing small increments of success. Will you have to keep talking about them bringing their backpacks to school every day when that is the expectation for all students? Not forever, but that is where you need to start. Eventually things that were hard will not be hard anymore, and you will start to recognize larger accomplishments.

An Extra Dose of Adult Relationship: Secret Mentors

For your especially spirited children, think about organizing a Secret Mentor program. Each staff person should plan to have at least two mentees, depending on the needs of your school. If you have 40 staff members, you have 80 kids who can get a little extra relationship time. That should be plenty to cover your most energy challenged students, as well as some of your next toughest group. Additionally, this program can be used to invite more positive relationship opportunities for your aides and other classified staff. Adults volunteer and children are assigned at random, so that new relationships are established.

Depending on the commitment of your staff and your school's needs, mentors can connect daily or weekly in different ways. Invite mentees to have lunch with them once a week. Make a point of at least checking-in with mentees every week. Author Stan Davis shared an idea called H.U.G. (Hello, Update, Goodbye) as a way to briefly connect with the student. Look for the student before or after class, make sure to find out how his/her day is going and give the child a little shot of inner wealth. Mentors can ask how things are at home, how the soccer game went, how he did on the spelling test last week, if they need anything or would he like to come by after school for help with homework, etc. It is best to keep this program under wraps as far as the students are concerned. Your challenging kids have probably already been involved in lots of programs to help them and may be resistant to something organized. Just having one person who really works on developing a relationship with them can make a student feel much more connected to school. Research has consistently demonstrated the strong correlation between the connection of significant adults and youths in regards to school success. (See www.search-institute.org/**assets** or www.resiliency.com for more information about developmental assets and resiliency.)

If a strong relationship develops between the mentee and mentor, extra time with the mentor can be a reward. Maybe getting to have a lunch brought in from some place as recognition for staying in class every day for a week, or being able to volunteer for a younger-aged classroom. Again, it is all about relationship.

UPHOLDING THE 3-LEGS IN YOUR CLASSROOM:
Exercises for Making NHA Your Own

So you have decided to make your classroom one where all energy given goes intentionally to what is great. You intend to step away from energizing negativity – you plan to ignore Joann's habit of interrupting and prepare to give her your attention the very second she doesn't interrupt. You plan to encourage participation from your sullen, quiet Robert by simply seeing him making an effort – and then naming it. For some students, you will be big and clear about their greatness, for others you will do it privately. You have decided. So how will this really work? You understand that this social curriculum – the relationship between you and the student– will happen regardless. The nature of this inevitable relationship is created by either positive or negative strategies. The warnings and lectures, the lens on whom ISN'T listening, sitting, working: that is relationship. It is an upside-down one, but it is still <u>relationship</u>. You, however, have planned to set kids up for early success so the opportunities for positive recognition are many, varied and endless.

These next exercises can help you in clarifying the climate and potential of a Nurtured Heart Classroom. Be warned to expect great results. Be prepared to be met with student skepticism and resistance to the new way that you are intentionally energizing them – and the whole class. Be prepared to feel great about your job and the progress your students are making, Timed-In to your energized classroom of capable learners.

Exercise #1: Teacher Questionnaire

Before bringing NHA in your classroom, it is useful to ask yourself some questions. Be as specific and thorough in your answers as possible. Talk to other teachers about your answers and how you might make changes to your room.

1) What would my class look like if it were just how I wanted it?

   a. How would my students treat me?

   b. How would they treat each other?

   c. How would they treat the room and supplies?

   d. What would we accomplish academically?

2) Which kids are almost always or even somewhat meeting my expectations?

   a. Academically?

   b. Behaviorally?

   c. Socially?

   d. In terms of how they treat their environment at school (desk, books, playground, materials, etc.)?

3) When children are meeting expectations, they are employing a variety of skills. For example, a child who does well academically must be motivated, organized, willing to put in the time and effort to do well, able to think critically, able to stay focused on a task (even for a short period of time), etc. What skills does a child need to meet my expectations?

     a. Academically?

     b. Behaviorally?

     c. Socially?

     d. In terms of how they treat their environment at school (desk, books, playground, materials, etc.)?

4) What have I said or done to let my students know when they are meeting my expectations? How do I recognize them?

5) What can I say or do to let these students know what their behavior reveals about their character and the skills they have?

NOW...Think of your three most challenging students and apply questions #2 through #5 to them. They are having <u>some</u> success just in the sheer fact that they show up at school!

6) Shift the lens and brainstorm ten positive skills these challenging students demonstrate.

7) How can you show these students that they are already being successful?

   a. What can you do?

   b. What can you say?

Exercise #2: How Would You Handle This?

Let's see how the 3-legs of the Nurtured Heart Stool would be established and maintained in some typical classroom situations. These situations can be fleshed out individually, or in teams, faculty meetings or small group discussions. (A cheat sheet of possible Nurtured Heart Approaches is at the end of this section.)

1. Starting your day

Take a minute to see yourself at the beginning of a typical school day. Students are walking into class. Where are you? What are you doing?

Nurtured Heart calls us to hold firm our space and the safety of the classroom, by what we see and name. Consider having a rule for your students that requires them to be in their seat, materials put away and starter activity begun BEFORE you answer any individual need or concern.

Katie enters the classroom. Rather than following the rule regarding the start of class, she comes up to you, interrupting your recognition of students on task and starting to work. She has a note that says she needs to leave early. How do you respond? How do you keep the energy positive?

2. What about homework?

Nurtured Heart demands consistency with rules. Consistent enforcement of rules helps students recognize their capabilities, understand the structure of their world and live within its boundaries. You have a rule that you do not accept homework after the day it is due. School is out each day at 3:00. Students, who do not have their work completed during the class/subject where it is originally collected, may turn it in by 3:30 at the end of that same day. How would NHA work in this example (based on a true incident shared by a teacher)?

Cory approaches you as you collect the last night's math worksheet: "Mrs. V, I don't have my homework. I did it. But last night my family got in this big argument. And then my older brother ended up running away, and he took my mom's car. And that is where my backpack was. I can get it to you tomorrow I hope – cause my brother came home this morning after I left."

Using NHA, how do you respond? How do you keep the relationship positive?

3. Establishing the rules

Consider the implicit rules of your classroom – and the expectations you have of your students working in groups, independently, as a class. What do you want your students to be able to do? Listen? Follow directions? Keep their hands to themselves? Share? What does it look like when a child is following the rules?

Using your vision of your NHA classroom, what might now be different about how you both set and <u>teach</u> the rules? What rules might you add and which ones would you change?

4. What should I do if a child won't reset?

You have taught your students the meaning of reset (not a punishment, but a chance to regroup back to the best version of themselves.) You also have demonstrated how to complete a reset in your classroom.

In the scenarios below, select the age group you teach (or try both) and challenge yourself to consider how you would handle the situation.

Younger age*:* Jose is a spirited boy, who often gets out of his seat, touches other people, or takes people's things. You have taught the class to reset by: _____ and Jose will do it sometimes.

(describe what a reset looks like in your class)

Today, he is particularly squirrelly. "Take-a-minute" you tell him, but Jose purposely ignores you and continues to wander around the room. Other students are distracted by him, but many keep working. What are some ways to get Jose to reset? What can you do or say if he will not? What is the consequence in your mind for not completing the requested reset? And what do you know you SHOULD NOT do or say to energize the negative?

Older age*:* Nina is a student who is consistently late, disorganized and basically not yet realizing her Q.O.G.s. In class, she repeatedly talks to her neighbor and is off task today. You reset her by:

_____. She rolls her eyes and pretends not to
  (describe what a reset looks like in your class)

hear you. She continues to speak loudly to her neighbor during your whole class instructions. You ask her to move to the table at the back until she is ready to work. She refuses to get up. What are some ways to get Nina to reset? What can you do or say if she will not? What is the consequence in your mind for not completing the requested reset? And what do you know you SHOULD NOT do or say to energize the negative?

5. Supporting a child's good choices during transitions

Transitions can be particularly tough for many students, as they often lack structure, boundaries and consistent rule compliance. Consider the transition to get ready to leave at the end of the day – or end of the period. How do you keep the tone positive and set the whole class up for success PRIOR to the surfacing of conflicts or problems. Using NHA, what looks different now?

Exercise #3: Try This!

Each of these "teacher challenges" is designed as a tool to keep you on track in recognizing greatness. They are simple ways to be proactive and consistent, until the intention becomes habit.

1) Take the three most challenging students you work with each day. How many positive things can you say to them? Keep tally marks to chart the number of positive comments compared to the number of behavioral issues. What do you notice?

2) Do a three-day test. On one day, greet every person at the door and say something personal to him or her like, "Hi Lisa, what a contagious smile." Strive to acknowledge their unique Q.O.G.s, but simply noticing their earrings or a new top is at least seeing them on a personal level. Then on another day, greet those same students generally saying, "Welcome everyone" or something equally warm but impersonal. On a third day, stay at your desk and don't say anything. Take notes on what happens each day.

3) Take ten paper clips. Put eight in your left pocket and two in your right pocket. Whenever you say an inner wealth building comment (remember "good job/thank you" alone don't count), move a paper clip from your left pocket to your right. If you say a negative (including a reset) move a clip from right to left. At the end of the day, your goal should be to have the number of clips in each pocket reversed from where they were at the beginning of the day (eight clips in your right pocket and two in your left). Glasser would press us to simply have the inner wealth comments, so this exercise is designed to increase our awareness of leaking and also intentional recognition. Risky awareness. Go for the Gold.

4) Use several bright colored post-it notes and stick them in random places around your room, faculty room, grade book, top of computer, podium or desk where you teach, edge of a file cabinet, white board or bulletin board, etc. Use these as visual reminders to say or notice something going right in your classroom or with a student. Alternatively, when you see a bright post-it, take a minute to jot the student a specific note about his or her Qualities of Greatness which he or she is exhibiting in class at the moment.

Exercise #4: Tracking Your Ratio of Positive, Neutral and Negative Comments

We have never met anyone who says, "I just focus on the negative" when working with kids. We all think that we have positive interactions with our students most of the time. When we really scrutinize what's going on in an objective way, we may be surprised to find out that we are not as positive as we think. (We know we have found this to be true in our interactions with our own kids.) This is a simple tally sheet to do during one class period as a way to increase the awareness of your voice. Keep the table on your clip board or wherever you can easily mark on it. There is no right or wrong here. This exercise is only for you to get a better picture of how much energy you put into acknowledging kids for doing things right versus commenting on their goof - ups. Try to be as honest as possible, and be fearless in your self-scrutiny. If you are able to do this for more than one period, all the better, as this will give you a more accurate picture of what you are really doing.

Additionally, staff members can observe each other, and principals can use this form when promoting strong Nurtured Heart habits. If you are an observer, be sure to name specific examples of what you saw going right during the class session.

Using the table that follows, track your comments for one period and put tally marks for each of the following:

1) Good Job/Thank you comments (These are pleasant comments, but don't build inner wealth unless connected to a Quality of Greatness demonstrated in the behavior being noted.)

2) Meatier nurtured heart comments that build inner wealth (Cameras, Scrapbooks, Maps, Decoys). These can be as simple as "You've got your paper and pencil out." If you really go off on a kid for all the great things she

is doing, give yourself one tally mark for each action/trait you point out. For example your comment, "You have your supplies out which shows me you are ready to learn and a prepared student," would earn three marks.

3) Number of resets (Remember, resets are not punishment. If a classroom is consistently NHA, resets occur significantly less than the positive recognitions.)

4) Number of negative comments, eye rolls, warnings, etc. (Watch out for unintentional leaking such as giving a qualifying compliment – a "Good Job, but" or a "Much better than yesterday" statement. We have often viewed these as positive recognition, but in reality, they are loaded with negative energy. They speak to the child's past mistakes or deficits.)

5) Number of discipline problems/buddy room referrals.

Positive, Negative, Neutral: Tally Record of Comments

Teacher/Staff person: _____ Date: _____

Class period/setting: _____

Observer – if applicable: _____

Good Job/ Thank You Comments	
Meaty Nurtured Heart comments: For something like "You've got your paper and pencil out" give one tally. If you really go off like, "You have your supplies out which shows me you are ready to learn and….," give tally marks for each trait, etc.	
Resets Given	
Negative comments, including eye rolling, warnings, voice raised, etc.	
Discipline issues, buddy room referrals, etc.	

Comments/Observations/Personal Reflections

_____
_____
_____
_____

CHEAT SHEET
For Exercise #2

All of the following answers are suggestions only. The important thing is to remember your intention. Ask yourself, "Am I upholding the three legs of my stool with my response?"

Question #1

Keeping in mind that you want to stay focused on the positive, look around for people in class who are doing the right thing to get your attention. "Carolina knows just what to do when she comes in; she has turned in her homework and is sitting down. If she has a question for me, she can raise her hand." Ignore Katie until she starts to do what she is supposed to do. After she is in her seat, "Yes Katie, I can see you have something really important to share with me. I'm so glad you are in your seat."

Question#2

This is a toughie, especially with those kids who have really bad home lives. We want to be compassionate, but we need to uphold the three legs. That said, you should have another option available for students who might be in these situations. "I understand that things happen. The homework is due today, but if you would like to work on it at lunch or right after school and turn it in by 3:30, that is fine. I know it's a hassle to do it again, but sometimes that's what we need to do. You are so capable of handling this challenging situation."

Question #3

Just a reminder that having rules stated in the negative, such as "No interrupting," is very appropriate and helpful in keeping things clear and easy for kids to follow.

Question #4

The first thing to remember here is that a refusal to do a reset IS NOT ABOUT YOU. Do not take this personally because it is the child's decision. Additionally, do not be too hard-nosed about how well the reset is done. If the children look at all like they are getting themselves back on track, consider that a successful reset. Tom Grove tells a great story about a kindergartener who was having a very hard time. Out in the hall with the teacher, she was backing away from her and refusing to reset. As the child backed close to the stairs, she turned around to look where she was going. The teacher jumped on the opportunity to say, "Amazing! You did your reset, Chloe, and you have kicked out the grumpies SO fast." Remember, your purpose is to get kids back on track. It is NOT a punishment. Be sure that until children reset, you do not interact with them, and they do not participate in any class activities. (For example, if you are handing out papers, do not pass one to the child.) But be vigilant for signs that a reset is happening so you can draw them back into success as soon as possible.

Question #5

    The key here is to think about the behaviors you want the children to demonstrate and name these in advance. "We are going to science lab now, and I am going to be looking for people who are quiet and in a straight line." When you start walking, "Justin, Jose, Andreas, Katie were clearly listening to me because they are quiet and this line is SO straight! The principal would be so impressed if she walked by right now!"

SKILLS OF A STUDENT: Group Activity and directions

Rationale:

In helping teachers and others who work with children to develop a broader base of Qualities of Greatness (Q.O.G.'s), this activity pushes participants to brainstorm the skills and strengths necessary for students to accomplish even the minor duties of being a successful student. As a team, they take a simple task (being on time for class, waiting their turn, etc.) and work to come up with a list of skills it takes and what character traits they must have to successfully complete the task. Later they connect these admirable leadership skills to some of their most energy-challenged students.

Directions:

Divide the group into partners or teams of three. Distribute a slip of paper with the task named (see following page for possible tasks of a student). Introduce the activity by naming the task they are doing right now: Brainstorming ideas. What skills are necessary for participants to brainstorm? Creativity, risk-taking, cooperation, team work, motivation, intelligence, a deep understanding of an idea, patience, persistence, playfulness, respect for the leader, etc.

Then direct them to do the same. Tell them that each team holds a task that students accomplish each day, and ask them to brainstorm the Qualities of Greatness necessary to accomplish these. They may use an adjective list from this workbook, one of Glasser's books or one that you create.

EXAMPLE: Being on Time for Class? A student must: be organized, have a good sense of time management, the ability to multi-task, be a motivated learner, be respectful of authority, see the benefit of learning, be cooperative, be a team player, be responsible, be diligent, be resourceful, see the big picture, be compliant... and so forth.

Allow 4 minutes and then go around the room asking teams to name the qualities needed for the task. Add to their lists if possible. After this is done, point out that these are the qualities of leadership – and these are what we seek in all our bosses, our friends, our teams, our partners. These qualities of greatness exist in all of our students.

Adaptations:

The list of skills can be adapted to any grade level. In primary/pre-school: What does it take to sit in a circle at circle time? Elementary-What does it take to work independently? Middle/High- What skills are needed to take notes in class? Additionally, this activity can be done independently, taking core tasks of a student and brainstorming on your own those qualities needed to be successful.

Connection:

Now have them look again at the qualities they had brainstormed. Ask them to take a minute to consider the most challenging child in their classroom or in their building. Look again at the list. Have participants name the Q.O.G's exhibited by this spirited child. Take a minute in the room to have participants share their student's greatness with each other.

WARNING – nearly every time we have done this activity with adults, including parent groups, the adults want to begin with the "problem," and they start by leaking negativity. *Susie has trouble with directions and often hits ....* Whoa! We interrupt right away, reminding them that they are naming the student's greatness. Energy, zest for life, leadership, humor, creativity, problem-solver, etc. Go around the room and ask each participant to share a word or Q.O.G.

about the student. Make a second pass around the room. Say, "Who wouldn't want to have a student in their class who is all of these things? Who wouldn't want to work with someone or play with someone or teach someone with those skills and strengths?"

The intention of this last piece is to help the adult who works with the youth to shift the lens and focus back to what is going right and what a child's capabilities are – not his or her problems. You must see the child as great, before you can change how you are in relationship with that child. This activity can be repeated after challenging interactions, too.

What are the skills ALREADY BEING SHOWN when your student is...

1. ANSWERING AND PARTICIPATING

2. ACCEPTS A RESET OR TIME OUT

3. TAKING NOTES

4. ON TIME FOR SCHOOL OR CLASS

5. SITTING PATIENTLY

6. BRINGING MATERIALS/BOOKS TO CLASS

7. COMPLETING HOMEWORK

8. TRANSITIONING BETWEEN TASKS

9. WAITING HIS/HER TURN

10. FOLLOWING A REQUEST THE FIRST TIME

11. ACCEPTING DIRECTION/SUGGESTION

12. PARTICIPATING IN A GROUP PROJECT

HOW THE NURTURED HEART APPROACH CHANGES
THE ROLE OF THE SCHOOL COUNSELOR

In a typical school, a student enters the counselor/school social worker office with a PROBLEM. The problem defines the situation and we feel that we are empowering our students by giving them a safe place to 'vent'." How often have you been told that two children need a mediation, or this child is having an ISSUE? There is a lot of reinforcement for problems during these sessions. Kids get out of class, they get to hang out with nice people who listen to them, they get to be part of the big school drama, etc. Certainly, we are problem-solvers – so we move to solution-based discussions, and we become the problem-fixers. We "process" students by doing an in depth analysis of what they did, why they did it and what they need to do next time. Often, we go home at night feeling as if we have accomplished little more than putting band-aids on serious wounds. Students view us as the staff who LOVE problems, because we will always make time for them when they have one.

The Nurtured Heart Approach trains us to understand how upside down this is to our true intention of empowerment. Empowerment comes with the knowledge that we are capable of handling anything that comes our way. With NHA we do not give pep talks, but point to a child's past and current success. Showing children how well they are handling difficult situations, <u>in the moment</u> truly empowers them. They develop the belief that they are not only resilient (i.e.

Once they hit a problem, they can bounce back.), but they are also skilled in AVOIDING problems. Their problems do not define them.

For so many individuals, problems are the source of their energy. They focus on them; they create or move to them, they become them. The shift with NHA begins with letting them know, and actually proving to them, that relationship exists without problems. The children can be defined (for many, redefined) by their qualities of greatness, not their issues.

How might this shift look in the counseling office when a youth comes in to complain about being bullied or picked on? How might you begin the conversation? Certainly, some things do not change. We are compassionate and welcoming. But the shift occurs in what we pay attention to in the interaction. Here is a quick illustration of how this has shifted in Tammy's work as a counselor:

A student comes to complain. (This is the first roadblock we dismantle, as complaining in itself diminishes by focusing on problems rather than solutions. A student can have a complaint, but the energy is redirected toward her powerful abilities to move past the problem.) Let's call this 4ᵗʰ grade student Jimmy.

> Jimmy: Ms. Small, George keeps making fun of me. I asked him to stop but he won't. He makes fun of Malik, too.
>
> (Isn't that often how it begins? There is generally not much warm up to the problem. And as my door is open, no knocking or hello, either. Oops! Reset on my part: They know I am welcoming!)
>
> Ms. Small: Jimmy, it is so great that you are here to work something out. You impress me with the maturity it takes to solve a problem.

<u>Jimmy</u> (smiling, stands a bit taller): I know, I know – I gotta tell you what is great about me, right? ** (See "Helping Kids Name Their Q.O.G.'s" below)

<u>Ms. Small</u>: See, again you blow me away with your skills. Yep, give me three other great things about you, other than you are a great problem solver!

<u>Jimmy</u>: Ummm, I am a good friend, I am good at soccer, I draw well.

(Note: I accept nearly anything here, though I prod and then require students to give irrefutable evidence of this greatness. More on that later.)

<u>Ms. Small</u>: Wonderful. You <u>must</u> be a good friend because you are here and one of the first things you shared was in support of your friend, Malik! Jimmy, you have had problems with George before haven't you? (This may be the first time he has shared this – but I risk the common possibility).

<u>Jimmy</u>: Yeah.

<u>Ms. Small</u>: And you worked it out didn't you?

<u>Jimmy</u>: Sort of.

<u>Ms. Small</u>: Well, you haven't been in here to talk to me about it lately. So I am assuming you used some of those amazing problem skills to solve your past problems with George, and maybe others.

Jimmy: I guess.

Ms. Small: Tell me what ideas you have thought of to solve this problem (Note: I assume capacity, not lack thereof).

Jimmy: Well ...

And so it goes!

Helping Kids Name Their Q.O.G.s

Initially, when asking children to name what they like best about themselves or what they are proud of, they are often stopped short. "What?" They think, "I came in here to talk about what is wrong with me and life, and now I have to name what is right?" Another question counselors can use is *"Tell me three things that went well today/yesterday/this weekend."* Your discouraged learners may struggle – but try not to rescue them. Tell them you will wait. Or prompt them for something at recess, at lunch, during computer class. Even the fact that they are there to trouble-shoot a problem demonstrates that they have the courage it takes to tackle problems. Identify the likelihood that they have tried other strategies of their own before they came here to work with you (creative, motivated, persistent, and likely, a good friend). After they hit the hurdle once, you will find they can more readily do it the next time. I also have one of those great lists from Glasser's books on my wall and uncertain students can draw an adjective from this if they get stuck.

With kids who really struggle, you can get them started with basics like "Are you wearing your uniform?" or "What time did you come to school?" When they say they are in uniform and on time, you can expand on all the qualities they need to do these things (responsible, organized, determined, etc.). Even if they say they came late, you can ask them about what they could have done instead of coming to school at all. "You could have stayed home and hung out and watched TV because it's hard to come to school when you know you are going to be harassed for being late. This shows your bravery, conviction, drive, good choices." There is ALWAYS something you can point to that they are doing right. Once you have pulled them along, make sure you have the children repeat or expand on the ways in which they have been successful.

If the student tries to move back to complaining, work at naming his greatness and capacity and focus him once more on skills. Sometimes we write down the strategies she can use, or we role-play. You know this step. But the core difference here is that we don't need to rehash the, retell it, find blame, or re-ENERGIZE the problem. Simply energize <u>the person</u> who is capable of solving it. This is how we truly begin to empower our students.

You can likely see how this works when two students come in to complain about each other, or are sent by a teacher to 'work it out." Start by having each person name two or three qualities which he really likes about himself first; then ask the person in conflict to repeat what the other student just said. This intentional system is adapted in Tammy's *Peer Mediation Program* as it slows down the students in conflict and sets them up to be stronger listeners. If the second student is unable to paraphrase what the first student has shared, I ask the first student to repeat it. Then, of course, the second student names his or her great qualities, and Student 1 paraphrases what she has said.

<u>Counselor</u>: You two have had problems in the past haven't you?

<u>Both</u>: Yes.

Counselor: And you worked it out, too. Wow! And here you are using your skills to work out this issue. You could be pouting or looking away. You could have refused to do that first part I asked you to do (naming a great quality), but you didn't. This tells me you are so ready to put this problem behind you and work it out. I bet you already have some ideas of how you can solve this particular issue, don't you?

Student 1: Well, sorta – we could talk it about it with each other.

Student 2: But we kept arguing! (They look to me – and I look to Student 1 next.)

Student 1: (after a beat) We could take turns and not interrupt.

Student 2: I don't even care about this anymore. I just want you to know how much it hurt when you didn't include me with XXXX.

Counselor: Wow! This is exactly what I meant about your skills. You are not interrupting; you are keeping calm even though you are experiencing these strong emotions. YOU are working it out. And I bet you didn't even notice that we didn't have to bring up the problem even, just your ideas to solve it. And, you don't need me to do it!!

Sometimes, we will ask them to come back to us when they have figured out a solution. If they stay to work it out in our office or mediation hall, then we will have them end by naming a positive quality of the OTHER person before they leave. (All these adapted steps are in the Peer Mediation forms.)

Occasionally, you will have students who need to cool down before they are able to go through this process. In this case, you can have them write down what they handled well in the situation and what they could have done differently. Also have them write what the other person did well.

The expectation should be that interactions for problems are always kept brief. At the end of the day, if kids have been able to work it out, THAT is the time for extra adult attention, focusing on the success the child has been having. For example, "Wow, you two really worked out the disagreement you had all by yourselves. That shows amazing independence and responsibility!"

Academic/Behavioral Conversations
in the Counseling Office

Children are also often referred to counselors because they are doing poorly in school (behaviorally, or academically). Rather than asking what is going on to cause this problem, I always ask kids what they are doing right or what has worked well for them in the past. I find something to point out that I notice is going well, even if it is as small as the fact that they are at school TODAY. (Never mind that they came late and left their homework in their bedroom.) I then go through a similar process to the one above, prodding kids to see their greatness, while identifying ways in which they are successful problem-solvers. The interesting things about changing the focus away from the problems is that kids will often volunteer what is going on in their lives that they have been unwilling to talk about before. It is a bridge outside of the problem – and one which assumes existing capabilities, rather than flaws.

Here is an example of how this works: Louisa had a student who was identified as severely emotionally-disturbed. One day she cussed out the vice-principal. She saw her when she was waiting to go home, after being suspended.

59

Rather than asking what was making her so upset (as she would have done in the past), Louisa honored her for staying on campus and accepting her consequence.

> Ms. Louisa: "Celia, I'm so impressed that you are here. You could just take off and not deal with any of this, but you are here." (She had run away in the past, but I did not need to spell that out.) "I'm also impressed that you did not hit Ms. Vice-Principal, because you look really angry. You used a lot of self-control, Celia."

> Celia: "I really wanted to hit Ms. *Vice- Principal*, but I didn't. I know what I did was wrong to cuss her out, but I'm stressed because I had sex with my boyfriend last night and we didn't use a condom."

> Ms. Louisa: "Okay, so you are worried about this. I'm so glad you are taking care of yourself by talking to an adult who might be able to help. Celia, it takes a lot of courage to share something like that. Let's figure out what you can do."

It is amazing to us, how much more open students are when we don't push for information, but rather focus on their strengths. It's as if getting built-up by their capabilities gives them the strength to discuss their challenges.

This scenario also works with discussions about academics. If a child has three Cs, a D and an F, focus on the C's first. Once the child sees that s/he is already being successful, bringing up the other grades becomes less overwhelming. Invite them to come in and share progress with you by showing off a daily or weekly report in their more challenging classes. Be sure to lay on the energizing when the improvements happen, and encourage other school staff and parents to do the same.

When teachers and administrators ask you to handle a problem, assure them (in front of the student) that the process will be short. Further, tell them that you will share with the teacher/administrator what the student will be working on the rest of the day. Ask the teacher/administrator to honor the student later in the day for any accomplishments. For example, "Carmen will be working on speaking respectfully, and following directions. Please take some time to acknowledge her efforts." This extra bit of energizing is very powerful, especially for our "high-flyers" (those kids who receive the majority of the disciplinary referrals – and are conditioned for all conversations to be around what they don't do well – or to be short-changed with the "Good Job, but..."). Remember, as in shaping the behavior of Rover, look to name what is going right for this student in this moment.

The beauty of using NHA as a counselor is that you go home energized yourself. You are no longer just putting on band aids, you are helping children transform. If your whole school is using NHA, you will start to have fewer disciplinary issues, allowing you more time to go into classrooms. This provides opportunities to not only energize students, but teachers as well. Pointing out a teacher's wonderful qualities to the class often results in students piping up about what they like about a teacher, too. This can help give a resistant teacher a little push. There are also opportunities to point out to the room how well different students are doing (especially ones who are often in trouble). If a teacher says something along the lines of, "You should have seen him five minutes ago when he was out of his seat and off-task," you can respond with "At this moment, I see that he is in his seat, focused, and has a pencil in his hand." Even if the child is off-task, lower the rope, and comment on it: "Jimmy is here today and he brought a pencil." If the student starts moving toward being on task (which they often will when they are recognized), point that out to the teacher as well. "Wow,

Jimmy is sitting in his chair and starting to write. He's looking like a really serious student!"

It's important to be fearless here, because teachers can be very intimidating. The key is to do this in a way that will not alienate the teacher. If the teacher is resistant, be sure you have first energized the teacher before you start in on the kids. Again, if you can't find anything to say, start with the teacher's dedication to children and her desire to contribute to the community. Most teachers had this at sometime, even if they don't seem to have it now. You might try something like "It's hard to get here every day, especially after doing this job for a lot of years. You are so dedicated to these kids." You can say this in a very matter of fact way, but with a smile. Not everyone likes the "happy clappy" recognition, and it's important to show that you can do Nurtured Heart without being overly effusive. Just like the challenged child who has forgotten how great he is, teachers can often forget their amazing impact and gifts, too. Nudge them back to greatness gently.

In addition to building up your teachers, take the time to work on the administrators and classified staff. Administrators rarely get recognition (and often get a lot of criticism). Simply letting them know you appreciate their support, or you thought their column was well-written, their ideas in the faculty meeting were appreciated – *anything* you can note goes far beyond what they often experience. If you are able to nurture them, they will be that much better equipped to nurture the staff. Remember that whatever you draw attention to; you will get more of, in all these relationships.

Counselor NHA Questions for Consideration or Conversation

1) A student walks into your office unannounced and begins to explain a problem they are having with a peer. Using NHA, how do you respond?

2) A student is sent to your office with a note from the teacher saying they having been crying in class. They are not crying now, but it is evident they have been. How do you handle this?

3) A teacher calls on the phone to say they cannot handle a student. You know that going to the classroom will diminish that teacher's capacity to control her class. What do you say to coach her through this challenge?

4) Progress reports have just come out. The vice principal gives you a list of students to meet with regarding their failing grades. How do you keep these conversations from focusing on the problem?

5) A parent emails you to complain about mistreatment by her child's teacher. She states that it is clear the teacher does not like her son as she grades him more harshly and frequently snaps at him. The student expresses that he hates math. The parent does not know what to do. How can you support the parent, the teacher and the student in bringing out the best version of each person using NHA?

6) What are three ways you can nurture the administrators in your building to improve school culture and bring out the best version of these critical leaders?

HOW DISCIPLINE CHANGES IN THE
NURTURED HEART SCHOOL

What we are trying to accomplish when we discipline children? Do we want them to grovel and beg for forgiveness? Do we want them to learn from mistakes made? Do we want to put the fear of God into them and show them that WE are in charge? Practitioners of the Nurtured Heart Approach intend to empower individuals back to their own capacity for Greatness. You may have learned in the past that the root of the word discipline comes from the word *disciple*, meaning "follow the way." With NHA, the purpose of discipline is to show children <u>the way</u> to make amends for poor choices, and then the way to make better decisions for themselves in the future.

These constructs can be aligned with the concepts of Restorative Justice (although Restorative Justice is not an NHA process). Restorative Justice is a theory whereby a person who has harmed another person or a community, takes responsibility for - and makes amends - for his actions. The person who has been harmed explains the impact of the event. He then receives an apology and reparation from the person who has caused them harm. If someone is able to restore the relationship with the person he has harmed, a mistake can become an excellent learning opportunity. Additionally, the process can build inner wealth. If I do something hurtful to someone else, I feel bad. If there is a way for me to make amends, and I am honored for this, my inner wealth is built because I was responsible, capable, loving, stretched myself, etc. I am no longer stuck knowing I did this awful thing, because I have restored myself and my integrity. Research has demonstrated that "Restorative processes which foster dialog between the offender and victim show the highest rate of victim satisfaction, true accountability by the offender and reduced recidivism." (www.wikipedia.org/wiki/Restorativejustice 1/8/2009)

NHA and Restorative Justice deliver consequences with an opportunity (and with focused energy) for the student to recover his or her Greatness. With Restorative Justice, opportunities are provided for remorse, forgiveness and reconciliation. "Our present system of justice asks: "1.What laws have been broken? 2. Who did it? 3. What do they deserve?" Whereas restorative justice asks: "1.Who has been hurt? 2. What are their needs? 3. Whose obligations are these?"" (www.restorativejustice.org 1/8/2009) Past discipline models focus on punishment, blame and negative consequences. NHA and Restorative Justice make a positive paradigm shift to children's capacity to handle the responsibility of their choices.

Discipline with NHA is not about punishment, but about ways to get children back on track when they goof up. This can be a major stumbling block for people who are tied to the idea that "the punishment should fit the crime." If we slam children with punishment every time they mess up, we move them deeper into a negative portfolio. Remember that with NHA, we are always fighting to make children recognize their greatness, even when they make mistakes.

The teachers at an NHA school are the main source of consequences. The first consequence is always some form of "reset." Teachers can have their own words for resets, or the school can come up with a term for everyone to use. The important thing is that when children makes a mistake, they don't get a warning, they don't get yelled at, they don't get the eye-roll, they don't get a check on the board, they get some form of "reset." There is no limit to how many resets a student might get in any given class period. Initially, the high intensity kids may need to be reset many times in one class period.

Using Buddy Rooms as a Support Tool

If resetting a child ten times in a class seems too overwhelming, a good option is to have Buddy Rooms. Buddy Rooms are neighboring classrooms, where a child can go to regroup. Teachers agree to be each other's buddies before the school year starts. It is best if a desk is set up away from the rest of the class in each classroom. A folder should be at the desk with an activity such as completing a Peace Treaty (see end of chapter). Children can also bring class work with them to work on. A child is simply given a pass by the first teacher to go to the other classroom. The Buddy Room teacher does not have to say anything to the students, but can just indicate where to sit. Remember that our goal is to have kids in class as much as possible, so students should not be in the Buddy Room more than about 15 minutes at a time. When the students seem ready to return to class, the teacher signs the pass, gives them a shot of inner wealth for the work they completed, and sends them back to class. It is essential that the student be welcomed back with a clean slate. He/she has done his/her time. If you, the teacher, are still feeling furious, take a few deep breaths to give yourself a reset. Remember that the child's broken rule is not <u>your</u> problem to own.

In-School Success (Versus Suspension)

The next step after Buddy Room is in-school suspension, which can be referred to as "In School Success." Schools can definitely operate without ISS by using buddy rooms, and in fact, it helps increase time in class if there is no ISS available. On the other hand, it is useful to have other options to help kids reset and as an alternative to suspension.

Making ISS work can be very tricky because it is inherently leak-prone. The students who end up in suspension are frequently those who are needier. Sadly, schools tend to staff ISS or its equivalent with charismatic individuals who inadvertently energize the challenging child's poor choices. This can make ISS very rewarding with negative attention, at the same time pushing children toward thinking they are "no good" as they get lectures about how they <u>should</u> behave. The staff in ISS should not pal around with the students and should maintain the expectation that work will get done. At the same time, they should recognize students' accomplishments while in ISS as much as possible, so they build kids up. If a student is spending a lot of time in ISS, setting up special time with the ISS staff as a reward for *staying out* of ISS can be helpful. In this case, the ISS member should limit her interactions with the student and an alternative to ISS should be arranged. The staff member should encourage the student, indicating that she is looking forward to having the time with her when she is able to stay in class. In ISS, students can work on assignments, but it is useful for them to complete a form about why they are at school and other directed questions, such as what they hope to accomplish by being there. The staff member for ISS should be sure to give lots of energy to good answers and effort.

In schools, we may be limited by what our districts mandate for misbehavior. For example, many districts have a "zero tolerance" policy for bringing weapons to school. You can still employ NHA, even when delivering mandatory consequences. The trick again is *where you put the energy.* It is helpful to use the forms at the end of this chapter to make consequences more productive when they are delivered. When handing out the forms, be very careful to avoid negative leaks (see below), especially if you are dealing with a child who frequently tests your patience.

Look at the difference in these statements. #1 = a typical way to suspend a student, #2 = the NHA way:

#1. "Here we are again. You were doing so much better controlling your anger. What made you decide to throw the chair? Is there something else going on that you want to tell me about? You knew you would get suspended, so why did you do it? Blah, blah, blah."

#2. "I have to suspend you today for what happened. You'll be taking some forms home to work on, and when you get back I really look forward to seeing you reach the goals you decide to set for yourself. Do you have any questions?"

Remember with NHA, we want *as little* time as possible spent on problems. If a child makes a poor choice, s/he should not be rewarded by lots of adult interaction time right after the incident. Save the interaction for all the good choices you see once the child returns to school.

Here are two different ways of "welcoming back" a child after suspension.
#1 = what often happens in schools, #2 = the NHA way.

#1. "Oh, is your suspension up already? It's been so quiet around here. Now, we talked about how you were not going to screw up anymore, right? Do you think you can handle your anger? You know, if you get one more suspension you're going to be up for expulsion, and we don't want that to happen, right?"

#2. "We are so glad to have you back! I see you took some time to fill out all those forms, and I want to honor you for your commitment to making things right with Ms. Smith. Would you like to tell me what you decided about how you are going to make amends for what happened? I'd also like to know what goals you set for yourself so I can cheer you on. Do you mind sharing those with me? You said you want to not talk back to teachers. Well, you have been very polite with me during this meeting, and you have not talked back to me once. It looks to me like you are well on your way toward meeting this goal!"

It is imperative that all your staff are on board in truly welcoming children back to school. If people have the attitude of just waiting for a child to mess up, THEY WILL. Let staff know that children return to school with a clean slate EVERY TIME! Make sure to reset those staff members who struggle to do this, otherwise it is a set-up for the child. The attached reparation forms and the Restorative Justice process should be helpful in combating this problem, but it helps to remind everyone that we are fighting for all our children to be successful, no matter how much they drive us crazy. If you have a teacher who is too angry with a child to really welcome him back, it is important to have a meeting with the teacher and student to work that out.

The following forms have explanations about how to use them most effectively. It may seem like a lot to deal with every time a child is suspended, but the initial investment will have big pay-offs with reduced suspensions in the future. All of these forms can be adapted to fit your school needs more closely.

How to Use the Discipline Forms

With each of these forms, you will need to talk to parents about the expectations, as well as the purpose behind each form. When meeting with parents, be sure to talk about specific things the child has been doing right. Congratulate the parents on being so committed to the child that they are willing to come to school in the middle of the day, etc. Parents of highly spirited kids may be particularly distrustful and resentful of the school. Use whatever you can find in the moment to point out their successes. When the parent comes for a return to school "interview" after suspension, be sure to comment on the child's successes in the moment as well. If parents are unable to come to the school for the interview and you must do it by phone, you should still follow the same principles.

Remember to be very careful to avoid any leaking when reviewing forms with students and parents. Your goal is to not put attention on the problem. Watch yourself for comments like, "I'm glad you decided to work on being respectful to your teacher. That's definitely something you need to do". Instead, try for comments like "I see you wrote that you are working on being respectful. You are being so respectful right now in my office and I want to recognize you for that. I'll be looking for you later in the day so I can honor you for this again."

1) *Let's Get Back on Track:* Suspension Form

    This document is adapted from a form developed by Tom Grove. It is pretty self-explanatory. The important thing is to make sure the child gets recognized for what s/he is working on when they come back to school and for the hard work s/he did in completing the form.

2) *Opportunity for Restorative Justice*: *Teacher/Student* Form

    As an administrator or counselor, trying to get a teacher to use this form may be the most challenging. Encourage teachers that we want to guide our students toward an understanding of how they impact the world around them and how they can be the best citizens they can be. We all make mistakes, and it is important to be able to do something to put things right. You might encourage teachers to google "restorative justice" to understand better what you are trying to accomplish. www.restorativejustice.com is a good place to start.

Additionally, this form works well for students who have been impacted by the identified student's actions. This allows for the student's own capabilities to come forward – and create a peaceful direction for restoring the whole community and moving beyond the incident.

3) *Reparation Form: Student*

This form can be challenging for students, and younger ones may need help. Encourage parents to sit down with their child to help them through it. If you think the parent won't do it or will make things worse, you may need to help the child yourself. Explain ahead of time what you want them to do. Even young children understand the concept of repairing things when they are broken. Here, what is often broken is trust in relationship. Very often, the reparation they come up with is a lot more than something an adult would suggest.

4) *Parent Letter for Student Suspension*

You have to be very delicate when talking to the parent about what to do with this form. Especially if you have parents who have come from abusive backgrounds, the idea of NOT lecturing their child is absurd. This is a great opportunity to talk about NHA, Restorative Justice, and the intention of this approach. Encourage them to look into restorative justice, if they have access to the internet and you think they will be able to understand the information on the websites. Give them information on Nurtured Heart Approach. In the teacher comment section, you can set up a chart for different class periods for a child in middle or high school. The teacher in each period can just write one of two words per day. Make sure that teachers follow through on this piece. Ask to see the chart every couple of days so you can congratulate the student as well.

5) *The Peace Treaty*

This form, adapted from Susan Zola, certified NHA trainer and award-winning principal, can be altered to fit a specific situation. It is particularly helpful in avoiding draining adult detective work – in that the child spends the energy writing – and rebuilding time-in after an altercation with another student or students.

<u>Let's Get Back on Track!</u>

So, you broke a rule or made a mistake in some way and you have been given a consequence. This is a big opportunity for you to figure out how you might do things differently in the future. We really do want to support you in being the best student you can be, so we are asking you to answer these questions before you come back to school. Completing this form is a powerful and positive choice. It shows that you are taking responsibility and are willing to take steps toward respecting your environment, your peers, school staff and yourself.

<u>Respecting Yourself</u>

Let's start with you. You are a VIP, a Very Important Person! Everyone at this school has a really important job to do.

1) List all the jobs you think people do every day:
   (If you have trouble remembering, just think about all the people you see from the time you get to school until you leave to go home for the day.)

What is your really important job that **you** do each day at school? It is your most important job in the school. Your job is to turn on your creative brain and learn all you can from the adults and your peers at our school.

2) Write down what you do for your job at school:

So, how do you respect yourself? There are several ways you show respect for yourself:

- Taking pride in what you do
- Using your words in a KIND way
- Taking responsibility for your actions
- Following expectations
- Respectfully and responsibly following directions from adults
- Keeping your "personal space" under control: your body, your desk, your stuff
- Being respectful of our shared school environment
- Using materials respectfully: books, pencils, paper, food, etc.

Respect for yourself also means you can be ready to try new things to keep from making the same mistake over and over. YOU CAN DO IT! Okay, you made a mistake. Now, you can find ways to fix it and <u>move on</u>. Isn't that better than dwelling on it? When you fix a mistake and move on, you can get back to your important job of being a student at our school. We need you here!

3) Write down three things you can do next time to avoid what happened this time:

1.

2.

3.

Respecting Other People

Do we have to like everybody? No, that would be great - but it is not realistic. But you can still respect people, even if you don't like them. Here are some ways you show respect for others:

a. Listening to an adult so you know what to do
b. Not talking when someone else is talking
c. Getting busy with your work instead of making fun of someone
d. Helping someone even though you don't agree with them
e. Saying you're sorry, if you say something hurtful to someone
f. Admitting you made a mistake, for example:
    "I'm sorry Mrs. Brown, I was talking and I didn't hear you. Could you please repeat your directions?"

4) List three (3) things you can do to show respect for others.

1.

2.

3.

5) Write about a time when you didn't feel like showing respect, but you did it anyway. What happened then?

6) When you return to our school, we want to support you as much as possible. What are some of the things staff can do to help you in your goal of being successful?

7) By completing this form you are already back on track to being a more successful student. Congratulations! We want to be sure to recognize you for the good choices you make. Name three specific things you will be working on that we can honor you for (for example, coming to school on time, not talking in class, being respectful to your teachers and classmates, etc.).

   1.

   2.

   3.

Opportunity for Restorative Justice: Teacher/Student Form

Teacher/Student completing form: _____

If a student has treated you in an unacceptable way, you may experience a lot of different feelings from anger to sadness. There is a concept called "Restorative Justice," which seeks to repair the harm done and restore relationships to all parties involved when there are very challenging/ upsetting events. _____will be completing a form before returning to school which will include his/her plans to make amends with you and repair your relationship. Please answer the following question, so the effects of the behavior are clear. Thank you!

What happened?

What was your reaction at the time of the incident?

How do you feel about what happened?

What has been the hardest thing for you?

Is there anything else you would like _____ to know?

What could _____ do to repair the harm done?

Reparation Form: Student

Student Name _____ Date _____

An incident occurred in which someone was hurt in some way by your actions.
You have received a consequence, and now have an opportunity to repair the
harm done. . An apology is always a good way to start repairing relationships.
There are many other things you can do, such as helping a teacher clean up after
school or doing community service, that help "make amends" (make things right)
and restore your relationships.   By doing this, you show that you are responsible
and making strong decisions for yourself - and on behalf of the people with whom
you interact. Please answer the following questions.

What happened?

What were you thinking about at the time?

What have you thought about since the incident?

**What do you think other people felt/thought who saw what
happened?**

What do you want them to feel/think about you now?

Who do you think has been affected by your actions? Consider your teachers, parents/guardians and peers.

How have they been affected?

What would you like to tell people to make them feel better about what happened?

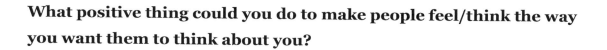

What positive thing could you do to make people feel/think the way you want them to think about you?

What will you do to repair the harm done?

What can you do to make our school a safer place?

A good way to repair relationships is to write an apology. Even if you do not feel sorry, think about what you could have done differently. Please write separate apologies to your peers affected by what happened, your parents/guardians, and your teachers. You will be given an opportunity to share these apologies in person.

Parent Letter for Student Suspension

Dear Parent,

Your child may have made a poor decision, but that does not mean s/he cannot be successful at our school. When your child returns to school, s/he will return with a clean slate, and we will expect great things! To help with this process, your child will be expected to fill out the <u>Let's Get Back on Track</u> worksheet BEFORE s/he will be allowed to return to school. We believe your child has received the message that what they did was wrong, and we hope that conversations around this issue focus on his/her strengths to move beyond this learning experience. We hope that any discussions you have will center on how the child will do things differently in the future.

As a Nurtured Heart school, we try to focus our attention on things kids are doing right. We believe that kids can often get the wrong message when they get a lot of negative attention for things they do wrong. With many kids, acting-out becomes the way to get noticed. When kids are recognized for the positive choices they make, their behavior starts to change. Please talk to your child about what s/he will be working on upon the return to school and ask about her/his <u>success</u> when s/he comes home each day. For example, if your child tells you that s/he will be working on not being rude to teachers, ask if s/he used polite language, kept his/her attitude in-check, followed directions, etc. Please honor your child for his/her accomplishments. Have your child fill in the chart below, and have his/her teachers sign it each day. By focusing on the good choices your child makes, we hope to gain quick movement back to her/his best selves once more.

Sincerely,

Dear Teacher (s),

I, _____ , am working on:

1) _____

2) _____

I would like your feedback on my progress. Please comment on my success.

Period/Teacher	MONDAY	TUESDAY	WEDNESDAY	THURSDAY	FRIDAY

School Peace Treaty

Written by: _____   Date:_____

Dear: _____,

When I was on the playground/in the classroom on (date)_____, here
is what happened:

It happened because:

I was thinking:

What I wanted to happen was:

The message I <u>thought</u> I was sending was:

The message I <u>really</u> was sending was:

This is who was affected by what happened:

This is how I will apologize to them:

Here are three (3) things I can do on the playground and in class to make it work:

1.

2.

3.

Here is how you (my teacher and other supervisors) can help me:

Here is how I will ask you for help:

Here are three (3) things I want you to know about me:

1.

2.

3.

Here are three (3) things I'm great at, that I want you to know:

1.

2.

3.

Finally, I would just like to say,

Sincerely,

_____

A Sample of a Nurtured Heart Discipline Plan

Our school strives to increase our students' sense of themselves as competent, successful students who make good choices. We employ a positive approach to discipline in line with the Nurtured Heart Approach (NHA), as developed by Howard Glasser. This approach builds our students' inner wealth by focusing on their positive behaviors and accomplishments, while providing immediate consequences for negative behavior. The purpose of NHA is to transform students' characters and spirits so that they are better able to cope with problems and succeed socially and emotionally. All staff members are vigilant about pointing out student success as they strive to be inquiring, knowledgeable, thoughtful, communicative, principled, open-minded, caring, risk-taking, balanced and reflective.

The Nurtured Heart Approach is based on three core principles:

1) <u>Pursue the Always Present Positive</u>: All people crave relationship and attention. Children often learn that the easiest way to gain connection with adults is through negative behavior because adults typically make time for problems. The Nurtured Heart Approach teaches children that they are able to gain relationship through doing things right. Our school staff strives to focus its energy and relationship on all positive behaviors. They have been trained to recognize that there is always something going right. They repeatedly highlight our students' Qualities of Greatness (character traits and behaviors which make each individual indispensible to our school). As a result, students begin to increase their sense of themselves as being successful and belonging to the school community.

2) <u>No Negative Attention/Leaks</u>: Little time and energy as possible goes into the attention on negative behavior. Students are timed-out for misbehavior; this is established not as a punishment, but as a way to refocus themselves and get back to the best version of themselves. There are no lectures or long discussions with school staff when a problem arises. Consequences are delivered swiftly and without emotion.

3) <u>Strictness</u>: The rules are the rules <u>every day</u>. If a student breaks a rule, s/he will be given a consequence immediately. There are no reminders and no warnings.

School-wide Discipline Plan and Consequence Spectrum

Our school-wide Discipline Plan is intended to protect the rights of our students. Students who demonstrate expected levels of behavior will participate in positive activities such as school dances, community building activities, recognition by school staff, positive notes/ postcards, positive phone calls home, special parties and other acknowledgements.

While in class, the goal is for the child to **remain in class** as much as possible. Students who break school rules should expect immediate consequences:

Level 1: Time out/Reset

What is a reset? For breaking a rule, a student is asked to "reset." The teacher tells the student to "reset," and nothing else. Students know the rules, and should not need an explanation. The reset is a quick and quiet reminder that the student is off task. Resets happen in the room and the student is to remain in his/her seat. A reset should be no more than 60 seconds. It is **not a punishment**, but a way to help students get refocused. When the student completes the reset, s/he is welcomed back and given a "clean slate."

(Failure to reset or continual resets will result in a pass to the buddy-room.) Resets may be given for the following:

- Gum
- Littering
- Distracting noises
- Shouting out
- Foul language (not aggressive)
- Excessive talking
- Disrupting instruction/learning
- Distracting behavior
- Out of seat
- Use of electronic device (device is taken away, put in envelope with name and given to _____to be picked up at a later time)

Level 2: Buddy Room

If a student continues to engage in the above actions, or refuses to "reset," he is sent to a Buddy Room. In the Buddy Room, she completes an assignment and is sent back to class. He receives no interaction from the Buddy Room teacher until the assignment is complete.

Level 3: Team Detention (10 minutes max)

Detention is given to students who refuse to reset. During detention there is no interaction with the staff member supervising the detention.

Referral Level:

Referrals must have specific details about the incident and what was said/done. Referral level incidents may result in suspension per district requirements. Students will complete our Restorative Justice paperwork.   Referrals given for:

- Bullying
- Overt defiance
- Disruptive/defiant/disrespectful for sub
- Truancy
- Vandalism
- Graffiti
- Verbal or physical threat (referral must have exact wording by student)
- Theft
- Fighting
- Aggressive/ demeaning language to adult (referral must have exact wording by student)

Referral, Suspension and Possible Recommendation for Expulsion (per district regulations for severe violations):

When a student commits a <u>severe</u> violation, administrative staff will assign consequences at their discretion. Our goal is to have our students at school as much as possible, so they are able to continue their learning. Consequences are based on individual student needs and the information/facts as they are presented, previous discipline history and prior interventions. Consequences may vary from incident to incident and student to student. Students will complete Restorative Justice paperwork. Severe violations are as follows:

- Physical injury
- Brandishing weapons
- Distributing drugs/alcohol
- Assault
- Extortion

INFUSING THE NURTURED HEART APPROACH
INTO THE FACULTY CLIMATE

One of the most powerful transformations of relationship often occurs when NHA is introduced and intentionally lived among the school faculty. Throughout this workbook, we have shared examples of Buddy Systems, Secret Mentors and some ways to recognize what is going right with our students. However, the most critical key to the success of NHA is the adult choosing to work with these students. Adults also crave this kind of recognition. There are several ways to bring the tools of NHA into your faculty meetings, as well as other opportunities for use with classified staff. The ideas named below are simply a starting block to making intentional positive recognition a cornerstone to all relationships in your school community.

The Nurtured Heart Moment

Making a shift in how meetings begin is a crucial element in renewal of attitude and spirit. And of course, what would be better than to make the shift to WHAT IS GOING RIGHT? Consider beginning each faculty meeting asking staff members to take a minute to reflect on their week and share something about a relationship or 'gift' shared by another staff member or a student. The moment of silence is a nice way to have us all stop in the varied demands of our job and actually THINK about ourselves as educators in relationship with <u>other</u> educators. Few of us do this job for the money. Most of us do it for many, many years. What is our draw if NOT relationship? Yet, often we are leaking negativity about our students, our staff, our administrators that is neither empowering, nor effective. Initially, only a few confident people will participate and share a Nurtured Heart Moment, but as the routine becomes consistent, nearly all will step up and honor a staff member or student. A teacher will share a story of how a colleague covered her class or figured out what was going crazy on her printer. Another will share how she overheard another teacher praising her classroom for their good choices – or how impressive the new bulletin board outside the north wing looks. The recognition is contagious, just as it is for our students; and honestly, rare to receive in a public setting.

Some staff will be reluctant to share – or equally embarrassed to be named. This, in itself, is a great opportunity for a discussion. Once staff gets in the habit of coming with a story, you will find that the mood of the meeting space is lighter and more congenial. Want to take it further? We have learned that when we recognize greatness in others, we are often seeing what exists in ourselves, but we don't often notice. As the leader, preferably the principal, taking an extra 30 seconds to add onto what the staff member has shared, really helps to highlight these qualities. John, the social studies teacher, shares how great it was to have his struggling student come to class yesterday with his project DONE! The faculty smiles and laughs; we know the student well. The principal then gets to add, "What a great reflection on your gifts as a teacher, John. You have never given up on Stephen!" BAM! The best tool we have in our teacher's tool box – awareness and recognition.

The Dilemma Discussion Moment

Our days are filled with quick interactions and resets. As counselors, principals and teachers, we could fill pages with amusing stories and challenging situations. We have included some common situations in the chapter on Classroom Structure, but taking one directly from a staff situation is a great way to have the staff come together as a team and practice using the legs of the stool.

Take a schoolhouse situation (faculty room gossip, hallway behavior, sending a kid into the hall, writing names on the board, resetting a girl who talks back, a child throwing a tantrum, tattle-tales, etc.) and personalize it for your building. Type up one of these situations on a slip of paper and distribute copies to smaller table groups.   Then have staff take 5 minutes in the smaller group to discuss possible ways to use the firm legs of the NHA stool in handling the common situation.

1) Positive Recognition

2) No Energy to Negativity

3) Strictness Adhering to Rules

If your staff is larger or you are working with a broad mix of grade levels, you could provide details or modifications for the situation. However, we have found that just working with ONE general dilemma each time seems to be a great way to have a common conversation – and to use common language. After the table conversations, ask for volunteers to share some of the ideas their colleagues brainstormed. This is again where we energize greatness. Educators are brilliant thinkers and amazing at creative solutions. Once they get used to this activity, they take greater risks in using the firm legs – or trying out an alternate approach from a past style. Tweak real issues (so as to protect a teacher's identity), in order to actually have genuine conversations around integrity and consistency as Nurtured Heart Practitioners.   The result is another opportunity for everyone to hear the strengths of the staff – and recognize the amazing depth of the learning community. The message you nurture: Everyone's gifts are valued here, and working together here ALWAYS WORKS.

Bringing Classified Staff on Board with NHA

Certainly, training all adults working with kids is essential for a Nurtured Heart School. In our fall start-up, we often encourage administrators to invite these key players to a "renewal" or initial training. This includes the very important front office staff – often the first faces to greeting students and staff with greatness. (Use our *Refresher* chapter as a tool to create common language and initiate dialogue.) Then in monthly supervisor meetings, you can also bring in specific schoolhouse situations which are related directly to their jobs as support staff. Using the 3-legs of Nurtured Heart stool, how do you handle...?

- Playground dilemmas
- Lunchroom rules
- Hallway expectations
- Helping kids recover back from a time-out at recess
- Not energizing when a child is sent to "The Office for a discipline issue
- Tone of voice when giving a reset or consequence
- Purposely energizing positively the next time you see a child
- Stepping away from 'gossip' about a child
- Reframing a negative snapshot that you placed on a child previously
- Coaching a new staff member with NHA
- Other situations specific to your school

Tammy began such meetings several years ago, and the climate among classified staff has improved markedly. These adults have a real role and a real impact on the lives of the children in our buildings, so taking the time to honor and hone their skills is key to building that climate of recognition. When all staff and students like to come to school, and feel recognized, they are more likely to recognize others. NHA is contagious.

Supplemental Reading Activities

Certainly using articles, chapters and selected stories from this workbook or the many books written by Howard Glasser and his co-authors is a great way to stimulate conversation and debate. We have used these resources at meetings or at follow-up trainings as fodder for the new "experts" (your staff) to answer in small groups and share as a whole.

Additionally, if a whole staff selects the *Inner Wealth Initiative* to read as a strong foundation for implementation into the school, key chapter questions can be added to keep faculty engaged (the Essential Questions we demand of our kids, too). *Possible questions follow at the end of this chapter for adaptation to your own building situation.*

Visual Reminders

Finally, having the NHA books (like this one), the core NHA messages, pictures or posters around the school and within the common areas where faculty gather is just a subtle reminder: "Welcome to the Nurtured Heart Zone. All Are Seen." "There is always something going right." "Step on up on your Greatness Pedestal." "Inner Wealth Built Here." "Got Greatness?"

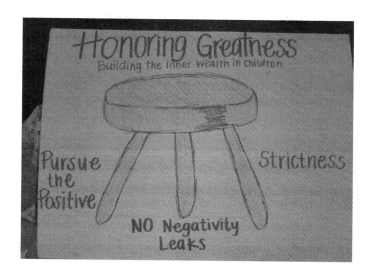

Tammy's high school junior daughter made a poster of the 3-legged stool for a speech in her English class last year. Even Tammy was surprised that her 17-year-old GOT IT! This symbol would be a great reminder in a building committed to staying focused on *What is Going Right*.

We distribute lists of positive adjectives (wonderful if they are laminated, too) to teachers and staff at the start of the year and each new training. Encourage staff members to keep the list handy and to expand the list with their own greatness. Louisa's librarian took these adjectives and made large laminated cards which she placed around the library for all to see, read and live. On a whim, Tammy taped up a copy of Glasser/Grove's Inner Wealth definitions in the women's bathroom last year. An anonymous faculty member even wrote a bit of graffiti on it: *Inner wealth is Staying Positive even when you are in the bathroom!* It remained up all year long and makes us think that is the kind of "tagging" every school welcomes!

Book Discussion and Reflection Questions

These questions can be used as a book study, separately or a few at a time in a meeting, or independently to challenge and build strong NHA skills:

1. The Nurtured Heart Approach (NHA) is all about the relationship between the student and the adult. Describe what you believe the intention of this system is in reference to the energy we give in relationships.

2. What are the Three Legs of the Stool in regards to the Nurtured Heart Approach?

3. How does the NHA differ from the quick idea that we need to "catch" kids being good to get them on the track to success?

4. Explain why children are so motivated by adult attention – positive or negative - as it might relate to one of your energy-challenged students. When have you experienced them pushing your buttons and when might you have been the prize in the classroom? When might you have unintentionally given rewards for negative behavior?

5. It is a faculty meeting. You are in charge. Using the concepts of NHA, energy and relationship, begin the meeting with a Nurtured Heart moment or strategy. Describe the moment here.

6. Right now, write down your biggest question in implementing the Nurtured Heart Approach into your classroom. Just let it sit here for a while.

7. What does TIME-IN look like in your classroom or when you are working with a child?

8. Give an example of each of the following ways to recognize a child in your care (based on definitions in our Refresher chapter):

   a. Camera
   b. Scrapbook
   c. Maps
   d. Decoys

9. Define Inner Wealth. Then describe in detail the ways students demonstrate strong inner wealth.

10. As a team, brainstorm the many qualities of greatness you have seen students demonstrate. Your staff as a whole should be able to come up with at least 40 namable qualities. Push yourselves to create statements of depth, in addition to shorter adjectives (i.e. "using creative solutions" rather than just "creative").

11. As the habit of naming what is going right becomes more natural, you will find a voice that matches your own. Looking at your brainstormed list from #9, highlight four of these statements which closely match your personality and which you could see yourself saying. Be prepared to use them the next day in class.

12. What is the core difference in delivering consequences with the Nurtured Heart Approach compared some of the other approaches you have used in the past?

13. Define a NHA reset. How might this work with your students – how would it look in your classroom, the lunchroom, the playground, the field trip?

14. Why is it critical to not give warnings and to be strict with rules... isn't this a Nurtured Heart Approach – all about positive recognition? Explain why these ideas are compatible.

15. What is a leak? Brainstorm common ways adults leak negativity. Consider backhanded compliments and comparisons to past behaviors/students.

16. Having forgiven yourself for 'leaking' negativity recently (let it go!), where do you think you can be a more positive voice in your building, relationships, family and students (i.e. what "leaks" are you willing to try and stop? ☺)

17. Consider an NHA credit system and describe how it could be used for an energy-challenged student in your classroom. Be creative. How do you introduce it? What earns credit? What can the student use credit for?

18. Taking all this into consideration, where do you see the greatest impact that NHA can make in your building?

THE POWER OF OUR VOICE: Group Activity and Directions

Rationale:

With each interaction and relationship, adults have the potential to make or break a child's day by the simple words they choose to say. This activity is a springboard to helping educators and other adults working with youth better understand the impact of their words. Often, before we use this group activity, we will ask participants to recall a time when an adult said something to them (either positive or negative) in their youth. Tammy will share a story of the reason she still will not draw people in her art work (her second grade art teacher's dismissive comment), and her decision to become a teacher (prompted by the positive relationship she had with her junior high English teacher). Participants will recall parent comments, teacher comments and coach comments which both drew blood or raised spirits. As educators, we may not really recall anything specific we said. But as children, who are just figuring out who we will become, we hold the powerful words of adults close to our hearts. The "never"s, the "always"s the "when will you ever"s, the "finally"s, the "I'm not surprised"s and the ugly tone of sarcasm. This activity brings a chance for us to consider the responsibility of our words on the hearts and minds of our youth. We can transform or destroy.

Directions:

Distribute the sheet with the teacher statements. Ask them to work in partners or small groups and to label each statement on a scale of 1 (meaning extremely powerful in destroying the inner wealth of a child) to 10 (incredibly powerful in transforming the inner wealth of a child). Tom Grove, from whom we adapted and added to this activity, introduces this scale a bit differently. He asks participants to consider labeling them from NGNWBAG to AGAWBG = or

"No Good Never Will Be Any Good" to "Always Good Always Will Be Good." This scale clearly names the heart of it: Our words and actions impact a child's inner wealth and ultimate resiliency.

Allow 15 minutes and an opportunity for good discussion. We would encourage trainers or leaders to add any statements to this list that their own teachers might have been overheard saying. Many of these are easy to label, especially the harsh and cruel statements. There are examples of leaking ("This is the last time..."). There are examples of simple demands ("I need you to sit down".), which are completely okay and a clear leg of the table. "Thank you for finishing your work..." sounds as if could be almost sarcastic. This is a great time to bring up the tone and intention of our voice. Certainly sarcasm can work to bring a classroom under control, as they all laugh with you as you ridicule a child for acting out. You win, but at what cost? As the statements are stand-alone (without background story or reference to the situation), many are open for interpretation. The key to this activity is the discussion around what we see and name. Sometimes recognizing that a child has simply finished his work is the first step toward his success. Each comment could be expanded to name more Q.O.G.s (Qualities of Greatness) giving the student irrefutable evidence of his greatness and keeping her eye on that prize. Additionally, you can adapt or add any statements to match your school audience, or overtly target playground supervisors, aides, office personal, parents, etc.

This activity is designed to increase our awareness and to make our words more intentional. We teach our students that they are 100 percent responsible for every action they complete and every word that comes out of their mouths. You can see how this transfers to resilient and powerful students when qualities are named, even when we are honoring self-control in a difficult situation.

<pre>
       1   2   3   4   5   6   7   8   9   10
Low Inner Wealth>>>>>>>>>>>>>>>>>>>>>>>>>>>>>>High Inner Wealth
</pre>

Rate the following phrases on a scale of 1 to 10:

(1 = greatly diminishes inner wealth to 10 = builds maximum inner wealth!)

1. "You are showing great creativity in organizing for this game."

2. "That shows you are really thinking about your options."

3. "What part of "Go get your lunch" don't you understand, Joe?"

4. "Even in a moment of anger you showed great self-control."

5. "This is the last time I am going to ask this table to quiet down."

6. "Your ability to work together shows respect and consideration."

7. "I am sick and tired of having to remind you to bring your coat out to recess."

8. "Brad, you are really using your internal control to step away from Tom and not hit him."

9. "Too bad this is your last day with the principal; this lunchroom has been real cooperative without you, Jane."

10. "Thanks for being such a valuable team member, Paul."

11. "I need you to sit down, now."

12. "Your kindness toward your friend did not go unnoticed."

13. "Good job!"

14. "You followed my direction the first time." (Consider: what could you add to increase your impact here?)

How Administrators and Coaches Can
Support Teachers in the Classroom

No one likes to feel evaluated by others. Even if we feel confident in our abilities to do our job, having someone watch us can be very disconcerting. A visit from the principal is especially stressful. This dynamic can make coaching teachers in using NHA very stressful. Unless you are the principal, or you have been assigned to do so, do not attempt to work with a teacher if s/he has told you s/he is not interested in your help. You are better off starting with those teachers who are receptive. Then wait for the word to get around that you are really helpful rather than a threat.

Before you enter a class, be sure the teacher knows you are only there to support them. At the first available opportunity, begin to build the teacher's inner wealth. Don't be afraid to interrupt the class (at an appropriate pause) to point out the teacher's greatness. You can also point out what you see in the students, but commenting on the teacher helps the teacher to be the prize in the students' eyes.

We find it most helpful to go in with a pad of paper and make notes as the class proceeds. You can also use the Teacher Monitor form in the Teacher Exercises chapter as a guideline. Add lots of inner wealth building comments about the teacher as the class progresses. For example, "You are so skillful at engaging everyone in the class. All eyes are on you!"

When something happens that might have been done differently, write what happened with a suggestion for how to change it. For example, teachers have a hard time giving up the habit of saying "I'm waiting" when they want the class to be quiet. (How long are you going to wait, and why are you giving that much power to just a couple of goof balls?) On the evaluation notes, you can write something like; "When you are trying to get the class' attention, try not to say "I'm waiting" because you want to be the one in control. Instead try, "I have

Tom, Javier, Sam, Leah and Deshawn with their eyes on me and their mouths closed. Thanks for your responsibility and respect." And when the rest of the class quiets. "Oh, look at that now I have everyone's attention! Super reset table four."

You can also make suggestions that are non-Nurtured Heart related. In the example above, you can suggest things to the instructor such as, "Consider saying, "Put your hands on you head if you can hear me." This will give you a quick visual and make it easy to recognize compliance.

You will observe some teachers for whom it will be very difficult to focus on the positive. Remember Rover and make every effort to name <u>small steps</u> toward success. You can always find something positive to comment on. Even their willingness to take in feedback demonstrates their desire to be the best teacher they can be. Once teachers start to have higher inner wealth themselves, it will be easier for them to build it up in others. Be patient. You might also suggest that they visit the classroom of a teacher who is doing well using NHA to get ideas.

Be careful to not allow yourself to be put in the position of "fixing" teachers. If they are not interested in your help, you are not going to accomplish anything. It is a waste of your time and the school's money to be in a class where the teacher is hostile to NHA, as some are. (Ironically, these teachers' spirits need the most nurturing. That should still be ongoing.)

For those teachers brave enough to do it, video-taping is a fantastic way to improve their skills. You can sit with a teacher and go through scene by scene to see where opportunities were missed, where leaks may have happened or when resets were not administered. Of course you want to point out all the good stuff and the teachers Q.O.G.s throughout. If a teacher is REALLY brave and willing to have the video shown to other teachers, everyone can learn. You can have staff watch the video and keep track of positive and negative comments and which way the teacher is directing the energy, as well as looking for places where things could have been done differently. Be sure you praise the teacher up one side and down the other so they feel the experience was worth the stress. This will make it more likely that others will step up to be videoed as well.

USING THE NURTURED HEART APPROACH IN
PARENT/TEACHER/STUDENT MEETINGS

Whether it is academic or behavioral, the Nurtured Heart Approach can transform the experience of all involved in these often challenging conversations. Anxiety is high for both parent and child. The child feels the pressure of the adult's expectations – and focuses internally on his or her shortcomings, rather than strengths. The parent waits for blame or a some new flaw to be revealed in his/her parenting. The parent's first panicky questions are, "What did my kid do this time?" and "What did *I* do wrong?"

NHA parent/student meetings are broken into three parts:

1. Identifying strengths (positive recognition)
2. Goal setting (without focusing on the negativity), and
3. Creation of a specific plan (consequences of the goals).

No energy in the meeting is given to the litany of the problems with the student.

When we begin these meetings, we start by asking each individual at the meeting to name what they like best about the child as a student in school. What are her best gifts/Q.O.G.'s (Qualities Of Greatness)? NHA staff is used to this approach by now, so each will come prepared to name several qualities and also give evidence to this greatness. We have coached them to step away from the leaking phrases like "When he tries, he can..." or "On good days," etc. These are backhanded recognitions that diminish the message of capacity – and pokes at the possibility of this, versus the certainty. Parents often have to be coached in this direction, also. With the older child, we will often meet with him or her prior to the meeting to reduce anxiety. We outline the objectives (<u>always</u> specific goal-setting and solution-focused) and hold the student to the same task: they, too, will have to name a Q .O.G. (Quality Of their own Greatness). They must fearlessly embrace their gifts.

Teachers, student and parent might name Q.O.G's such as intelligent, motivation, curiosity, insight, persistence, determination, ability to follow rules, supportive to peers, engaged, focused, etc. The Q.O.G. is followed by a story which reflects the demonstration of this strength.

After 'greatifying' the student, we then ask the teachers to do a second go-around of what specific goal area they want to have the student address. They choose only ONE area of improvement such as: increase focus, OR better communication, OR no more missing work, OR ask questions in class, OR handle resets, OR reduce distractions, etc. Student and parent also participate in naming the goal they seek. From there, we get more specific to provide the tools to address this. The support for the goals comes from the initially named Q.O.G.'s.

Here is an example session of a NHA meeting with a student named Cory, who was struggling academically and behaviorally in his classes.

After introductions, we begin with the first stage:

1) <u>POSITIVE RECOGNITION</u>: In the directed 'go-around', Cory's teachers say that he asks really great questions, and shows strong intellect and curiosity.

Cory is a strong writer. Cory is respectful and accepts consequences with maturity. Cory is a natural leader in the class, and students and teachers like his happy, upbeat personality.

*NOTE: Cory was failing two classes. He did not turn in his work. During independent work time, he often distracted classmates, or simply doodled, dawdled and let the time go by. His work was incomplete most of the time. NONE OF THIS WAS SAID - because Cory knew it. Mom and Dad knew it. We knew it. Everyone knows **the problem**. What we were there to do was to find THE SOLUTION. Cory's problems were not the solution. Cory's strengths were.*

2) GOAL SETTING: At our second go-around specific goals are named. Cory needs to use class time. Cory needs to complete his work. Cory needs to ask for help when he is stuck, and use his teachers and "smart" students (those on task) for help/support.

3) STUDENT PLAN: Cory's friendly nature and respectful maturity make the task of asking for help a natural first step. We set a day before and after school (voluntary force ☺) and also name two kids in each class that Cory can seek out for help in class or from home on the phone. On the final written plan from this meeting, these student names and numbers are included. The use of the planner is critical in communication between home and school. It's easy to do - and now it is tied to the positive consequence that each Friday he can have extra computer time IF he successfully completes his planner all week. Because Cory admits that he is capable of getting his work done, the teachers also agree to no longer take any late work from him. Cory acknowledges that the NHA's strictness to the RULES will help him, too. Cory is given the leadership responsibility to write down the daily assignments on the board for the whole class. *The plan will be revisited after four weeks, and his counselor will meet with Cory during his lunch recess on Thursdays to check in.*

At the end of the meeting, we reiterate Cory's qualities of greatness which will help Cory be successful, adding, "Isn't it just awful to have all these teachers tell you how capable, skilled and great you are?" The parent smiles too, and adds, "Can I go next?"

There are times when the teachers or parents may have a very hard time identifying student strengths when they are mired in what is going wrong. You can help them by beginning with "I have noticed..." or "Isn't it true that..." Be prepared to coax the greatness out – even of those parents struggling. Acknowledge the parent/teacher for awareness, for being focused and motivated, encouraging and intentionally positive in the direction of the meeting. Give advanced notice to parents, teachers and even the student that you will be asking them to name their strengths. For parents, this often reduces the anxiety they already experience when coming to meet with teachers, and for the child it is a breath of fresh air. Everyone knows the ways and details in which the child is stumbling. Reminding or spending any time on this will only derail the objective of solutions and the skills the student ALREADY POSSESES.

(See **STUDENT SUCCESS MEETING** form. Staff unable to attend can complete the three sections with feedback prior to meeting – as can the student to prepare in advance for the meeting – and increase the student's confidence in his/her own ability to be successful.)

Student Success Meeting

Student Name _____ Grade _____

Date: _____ Point Person (completing form) _____

Parents/Guardians attending:

_____

Teachers/Staff Present (subjects):

_____

_____

_____

Student's Qualities of Greatness:

Goals for Success:

Specific Plan for Achieving Goal connected to student's strength/skill
(i.e. Using Planner daily (motivation, strong communication):

WHAT ABOUT THE PLAYGROUND?
Simple Tips for Bringing NHA to Other Schoolhouse Settings

As mentioned in our chapter on staff and faculty ideas, empowering and educating all staff who interact with students using the Nurtured Heart Approach is essential to establishing a consistent climate where positive recognition is at the core.   While each building has unique protocols for playgrounds and lunchrooms, a couple of common elements can keep the legs of the stool firm – and ensure kids feel great about coming to school.

Some Ideas for Playground Staff

- You have one of the best jobs in the school – your job title starts with the word "Play!" Monopolizing this positive energy, allows you to be seen as someone accessible and friendly. Make it your objective to learn five names every day. Names are a key way to connect with kids and help kids seek out your powerful recognition.

- You are critical to kid's safety. You can provide opportunity to name what is going right as your first interaction to a child's game or cooperative play.

- Praise notes or other forms of written recognition are a great way to have staff circulating on the playground, looking for what is going right. The Peacebuilders Program uses these, and Tammy's school created its own carbonless versions, so that the second copy can be placed into a box for extra rewards or publication of names in our newsletter.

- Consequences should be brief and without lecture or warning. A child pushes out of frustration, remove her from the game: "Oops, broke a rule. Sideline." One minute. Then back in the game with ample opportunity to prove her greatness.

- Tattling is a common communication on the playground. Help children be empowered by asking what they did to solve the problem. *"You came to me! Wow, what a great problem-solver you are! What do you want to do now? Play another game? You are so resilient. You sought a wise person. You solved your own problem."* These are the messages we want kids to get. If we play detective, we inadvertently give energy to the problem and do little to empower the child. He stepped away. He came to you. The problem is already over. And he has the tools to handle this.

- Consider having minor incident reports. These are simply running records staff can use to make notes about an incident or child. If a "frequent flyer" name appears, it can be a great flag to build that child's capabilities PRIOR to a discipline referral. All specialists and classroom teachers can use these forms. (These incident reports are given to a principal or VP to enter in a database, and then shared at regularly scheduled supervisor meetings – or with a counselor monthly.)

- If you have had to consequence a child the day before or even had to write a discipline referral, seek out the child at the next available recess to reestablish positive relationship. *"You handled that consequence with great maturity. I really like the way I see you playing basketball with your class today."* If the child has a history of peer issues, your goal to catch him as he comes out to the playground every day, first thing, will go far in helping him shift his self-portfolio. Camera comments like *"I see you playing with John."* or *"You are taking turns."* can often be as powerful in building his capability as can Scrapbook statements such as *"You are doing a brilliant job waiting in line. What patience!"*

Lunchroom: Kids 2nd Favorite Place

- As in all the suggestions above, this environment of chaotic structure ☺ is a great place to build the inner wealth of children. Responsibility is a core quality that should be nurtured here. Recognize the skills needed as students demonstrate respect for others, sharing close quarters without responding aggressively, following directions in a large, mixed environment, and being welcoming to other students.

- Taking every opportunity to name what you see going right will give you more of that. And as all seek this attention, others within earshot will reset themselves to be seen.

- Catching kids at the lunchroom door with Maps of their greatness will get them moving to follow the rules, because when they do, they are seen.

- Many lunchrooms offer credits, class bonus points or individual "early dismissals" for exceptional responsibility.

The intention in these interactions is energy toward positive recognition, rather than inadvertently rewarding negative choices with more relationship.

The Bus: Ride to Greatness

Bus drivers are often the first school adult to interact with students each day. The potential of this first connection is critical in setting a child up for a successful, powerful day. Empowering and honoring the drivers with skills to build capacity in the students they transport is an essential tool for creating the driver's buy-in to the Nurtured Heart system of relationship. Consider training these powerful cadre of para-educators in your school in-service days, and energize their role in creating a positive beginning AND end to the school day.

- Many of the suggestions for other school settings can be easily adapted to a bus setting. While safety is an issue that cannot be overlooked, what we learn with the Nurtured Heart Approach is that building capacity to follow rules comes from naming what is going right, and honoring the students who buy-in to the rules and comply. Students are much more likely to give you more of whatever you name and energize. So name the rules that are being followed recognize the students who are cooperating and groups that are quick to reset themselves.

- Remember that broken rules are not about you (unless you give them energy). Assume greatness first, and that the child simply "forgot" their Q.O.G.s for a minute. "Darn, broke a rule." Then when you reset the student (or even better, recognize when they reset <u>themselves</u>), you can welcome them back quickly to your positive relationship.

- Learn every child's name and don't hesitate to ask he/she to repeat it again every time you greet him/her. The message they receive from this intention is, "I am important. I am seen. I matter."

- Often bus drivers only rise out of their seats to address safety issues. Consider an alternative impact of your presence where you might stand to greet incoming students, turn to smile or recognize kids in the back rows.

- Name the sharing you observe. Honor students for moving over for others, not pushing when they come in, keeping voices down. All of these Camera and Portfolio moments will have the greatest impact if you use their name. Names are everything. Positive nicknames, especially, can be such a great tool for highly spirited children as they indicate a special relationship. I see you. I see you as special. *"It's Enthusiastic Emily! And here comes Creative Craig, too. Way to be so respectful when you enter the bus,*

Brave Barry." Using nicknames or matching adjectives to their first name will actually help <u>you</u> to remember their names, too!

- Consider cool stickers for a recognition tool or even creating your own credit system where kids earn privileges (i.e. singing a bus song or telling an appropriate joke to the whole bus, being the first on, or choosing a special seat for the "rider of the day", etc.).

- Use the list of positive adjectives and keep them handy so that you are reminded to name the successes you see.

Finally, for <u>all</u> the adults who connect with students during the day, take advantage of the opportunity to build positive relationship with children, even when you are "off duty." Work to know and say their names: you will be surprised how pleased they feel when you remember. Complimenting the good behavior and the good choices you see as the student moves in the hall, lines up for the bus or heads out for gym is particularly powerful when you are <u>not</u> in the role of supervisor. Never underestimate the power you have with a simple Camera or Scrapbook observation to transform the way a child feels about his/her day (nor the power of your welcoming smile).

RUNNING CLASS MEETINGS:

Bringing Out the Best Version of Your Classroom

When Tammy was in her Masters program, she learned a great deal about William Glaser – a renowned psychologist who was famous for creating a dynamic model for class meetings. Stepping into the Nurtured Heart Approach, it was easy to see how using his system matched Howard Glasser's relentless pursuit of the positive.

The purpose of class meeting is to promote a connection between students and to build a strong classroom community. Meetings can focus on a character-building lesson, inclusive group social skills, or problem-solving strategies related directly to student issues in the school. Using a bibliotherapy model, the leader could read a thought-provoking book or article. Alternatively, she could bring in a school or current issue for a discussion of values clarification and student integrity. In the many years we have led class meetings and coached teachers in this system, we have yet to meet a child who does not look forward to the meeting: Okay, perhaps it is because they may be missing a math lesson. The best part of every lesson is the last 5-8 minutes of energizing, in which the students to recognize the Qualities of Greatness (Q.O.G.'s) in their classmates.

Establishing the Routine

Students move chairs into a circle, seats are random, but students are positively recognized for choosing to sit next to someone who will help keep them focused.

In the first session, we create "Ground Rules" for class meetings. Students volunteer rules that they think will help each class member be fully present. Accept all answers, even repeated ones. Rules that are stated in negative such as "No interrupting" are welcome reminders of clarity. From preschool to high school, we have found that these established rules are amazingly unvaried. Students know the rules – they like the rules. Rules, and compliance with them, create a stronger place of trust and safety (key elements in successful class meetings).

Ask, "What should we do if someone forgets how great they are (*a phrase Tammy often uses when she explains resets or time outs to students*), and they break a rule?"

Accept answers, and help students remember that most rules are broken unintentionally; however, without a quick "reset" some students would not have a chance to step back to their greatness and fully participate as the best version of themselves. Often, Class Meeting Guidelines for older children will include a simple rule like, ACCEPTS RESETS WITH MATURITY. Modeling what this looks like in a circle is necessary, so we often reset the whole class. This is a great chance to recognize students for following directions, acting with great self-control, responsibility and respect.

Later, type up the class meeting guidelines, laminate and post them in an easily accessible location in the classroom. Begin each class meeting by having students read the rules aloud, one at a time, pausing to do a silent, personal agreement to try their best to follow them.

Tools for Discussion/Curriculum

This model of conversation can be used with character education curriculum, like Committee for Children's *Second Step* or *Steps to Respect*. It can be brought into religion classes, life skills courses, alcohol and other drugs information formats, or healthy choices programs.

Many teachers use this format to have students come up with their own topics: Handling bullying behavior, eating disorders, internet safety, preparing for the next year, resolving conflicts, handling anger and other strong emotions, etc.

Using books or current events as topic starters will engage students into strong debates and honest dialogue. Some classes use journals so that ALL students participate, though not necessarily aloud.

Once the model is established, a group of students or a classroom teacher can call a class meeting if a new issue arises (a sudden serious illness or absence of another student, a heated conflict on the playground, a new policy set forth by the school, etc.)

Energizing the Greatness

This portion is by far the favorite of nearly all students. One can see how you could take a whole meeting to simply go around and say what is great about each person in your class. When we do this the first time, it takes longer – and you can consider providing students with adjective lists to help them get more creative in naming qualities of greatness.

Use a small stuffed animal (perhaps a Beanie Baby; Tammy has a small bumble bee which she coins her "BEE Positive" ☺), but any easily tossable item works well, as even high school students still love stuffed animals! A student will raise his hand to share a positive quality. Toss him the BEE – and they will begin, "*I want to energize/compliment/etc... XXXX*"

Students are instructed to say something great about another student in the classroom. They are called to name the great quality, and give irrefutable evidence of this greatness. *(EXAMPLES: Jodi is a great friend because she makes me laugh when I am down, and she took me to the nurse when I felt sick yesterday.* Or *Kirby is such a talented artist. Her picture of the flowers was just amazing.* Or *Bobby is a great team player. He doesn't get mad and he includes everyone.)* We are always amazed at how quickly they learn to do this.

We eliminate words that seem empty (like "nice" – as everyone is), and then I will sometimes have to ask a student to elaborate. When she has completed the statement, she tosses the BEE back to us, and we toss it to another student raising his hand.

Each person can only be energized once a session, though we are quick to tell students that they can always go up to a student later and give him/her that compliment. Who doesn't want to hear about their greatness? Students can only compliment one person at a time; however, they may raise their hands later to energize another student.

When we first begin this, we require that each student be energized. Some of your students will be gifted in recognizing greatness in every student. Sometimes, we will ask students to energize a person for a quality that was the focus of the lesson, such as tolerance or welcoming. (i.e. *Who can name someone in this class who showed great patience this week?)* Occasionally, we will energize a student ourselves. If we have seen some great transformation between this lesson and an earlier one, a step-up in maturity or a level of engagement where it seemed lacking earlier, then these character qualities call to be named. (i.e. *"You really stepped up this meeting, Karina. You brought such great insight and compassion."* Do <u>not</u> add: *So much better than last week.)* No leaking of past behavior – just honoring the greatness seen.

We have rarely had to reset a student during this time period, as participation and focus is high. We will sometimes need to interrupt an energizer for 'leaking' (*I want to compliment Bart 'cause when he says he is sorry, he means it. Sometimes.*) Those are actually great conversations in themselves about valid compliments – and empty ones. And a great call to students: *If they can do this once, they can do it all the time.*

Bringing closure to the energizing is hard – even for us. Greatness is addictive. But math class is great, too, so helping the students transfer this enthusiasm is a good test of your own ability to not leak! ☺

**BYSTANDER EMPOWERED: Using NHA to Address
Peer Relationships and Bullying**

Every school is required to have an anti-bully policy. Schools take bullying seriously. We want kids to be safe. Safe kids are less stressed – and less stressed kids learn more easily. Most bully behavior, however, flies under the radar of adults. Additionally, these behaviors are often dismissed, lectured, warned about or even excused by the very adults who exist to keep kids safe. These programs fail in two ways. Kids are not scaffolded in their qualities of capability at the level needed to stand up to the social risks required to intervene in bullying. Secondly, many schools do not enforce broken rules of peer mistreatment with the same level of seriousness or consistency needed to eliminate the behaviors. Again, we come back to a Nurtured Heart School and how things are different.

The Nurtured Heart school builds the inner wealth of children, and therefore the resiliency of children. The Nurtured Heart Approach also insists on compliance to rules and no energetic relationship when rules are broken. We hold kids to high expectations because they can do it! The authors have evidence that when children truly believe in their own greatness, they will not become bullies, or targets of their peers. Recent research contradicts this stand, implying that bullies actually enjoy strong egos and firm self-esteem. While we are not in a position at this publication date to cite contrary information, our combined 45 years of working with challenged youth has formed a different hypothesis. That may be our next adventure – because all identified bullies we have worked with lack skills and REAL belief in their own greatness. Outside of the sociopath (and yes, we have met a few of these, too) both of us have had transforming experiences with children wanting to be defined differently, by first helping them define themselves differently.

That aside, the Nurtured Heart Approach can be a huge catalyst in eliminating the existence of bystanders, those who stand by and watch others being mistreated in schools. Using a class meetings format, or one of the essential springboard questions that follow, teachers and even students can lead powerful discussions which challenge people to step up to their greatness. With the use of real historical examples, coupled with realistic student experiences, students can begin to make the mental and then emotional leap BACK to their intention. Nurtured Heart teaches us to know that character is all we have to stand on at the end of the day. Driving this home in peer situations is a tool for incredible insight and an opportunity for bystanders, targets – and bullies alike, to consider the intention of their actions.

NHA is all about relationships, and so are children. We thrive and live for them. We all want the same things: to belong and to connect. Keeping this at the center of your vision of children, see the bully. See the target. See the bystander. And see the social risk we are asking children to take. The bully's actions are motivated by wanting to belong and connect. The target's INACTION is motivated by the wanting to belong and connect. The passive response of the bystander, despite being disturbed by what they observe, is likewise the result of his/her desire to belong and connect. If we challenge a child's actions using his/her qualities of capability, we are pushing the child to risk the belonging and connection. And if we proactively build inner wealth – and reward this risk with recognition, we can see kids motivated to step up against injustice – and still belong and connect. The intention for school staff is to make the rewards for the bystander greater than the risk: praise notes, public recognition, credits for privileges, acknowledgment of the social risk taken by the student, "over-the-top" naming of Qualities of Greatness WHENEVER an adult observes a child stepping in to help another, etc. This should be the climate of a Nurtured Heart School anyway – but proactively energizing kids to be social activists will create contagious behavior. Whatever you see and name, you get more of.

Starting here, with this idea, you can tackle bullying and bystander behavior with essential questions which prompt the greatness of our character. Some follow here. Use just a couple at a time to promote greater depth of analysis. Pick a class recorder to take notes (a different one each time). Initially, you can have students write responses as journal entries. However, the intention of these powerful conversations is to move kids toward social risk – and still keep them connected and belonging. So building a child's confidence, creating safety, and modeling risk in the class meeting or group setting will help move each child to risk sharing – and therefore, changing. After an exploration of all students' gifts and acknowledgement of their need for support and inclusion, consider using all the insight and positive energy to create a class project. One possibility might be a class paper on what bystanders do at a Nurtured Heart School, another might be a mural of kids on a playground confronting a bully, another might be a book of poems about the gifts of each child – and how each member of the class supports each other. The creative ideas of your students will be limitless. The intention is to do something significant and teach social activism.

Questions for Engaging Bystanders

GOAL:

Use initial non-threatening questions to open up safe conversations around behavior in general. Many of these kinds of questions exist in books or other curricula. The difference here is that you are going to gather student's strengths, and use their sharing and risk-taking as tools for challenging them into stepping up to bullies (versus choosing to be a formerly non-engaged bystander). NOTE: SEE CHAPTER ON CLASS MEETINGS IN REGARDS TO ESTABLISHING CRITICAL RULES FOR TRUSTING CONVERSATIONS WHICH ENCOURAGE SHARING.

DIRECTIONS FOR LEADER:

Have each student come with a journal. Post one or two questions at a time. You could even have this as an entry activity for the beginning of a class or day – but then use it later in your class time.) You may want to have them share in small groups, as this will encourage all members to participate. Then come together and ask for some of the best ideas "Who can share a good idea or point that was named by their teammate?" After the ideas are explored and added to, take the details and help the kids name and expand on the strengths of character demonstrated in each example (being a good friend, a risk-taker, courageous, fearless, compassionate, friendly, tenacious, helpful, humorous, joyful, works for justice, etc.) Each week, begin the next discussion of questions by naming these qualities again, and with each question explored, continue to build on this list. These are the strengths that are core to a child's resiliency. They exist in all of us, and your intention is to empower these students to believe enough in themselves to take the risk to step up to injustice EVERY TIME.

Intentional Questions: Focusing on Peer Conflict

1. What does it mean to BE at risk? Give examples of situations in our world where communities or individuals are at risk.

2. Tell about a time you have taken a risk (physically, academically, or emotionally).

3. What might be an example of a social risk that a person would take at school?

4. Share a social risk you have taken (at school, on a team or in an activity with peers).

5. Is it ever okay to tease a person in a wheelchair? If it is never okay, explain why people tease others who are overweight?

6. Tell about a time you were worried for your own safety – or the safety of another around a peer.

7. Tell about a time you watched someone being mean to someone else. How did it make you feel?

8. Tell about a time someone stood up for you? What did they do? How did you feel?

9. Tell about a time you ignored a hurtful comment. Explain how you were able to do that without feeling bad the rest of the day.

10. A bunch of kids are teasing another kid in class. You can tell he is upset. Be honest: what do you normally do? What do you wish you could do? What would you need to be able to take the social risk to intervene?

11. Someone makes fun of you in class. Everyone laughs. How do you feel? What do you say or do?

12. A student in your class has a stutter. You have never heard someone stutter before and at first you think they are doing it on purpose. You laugh and copy them. You realize that they can't help it. What do you do?

13. Friends can tease friends about different things. What can a friend tease you about that won't hurt your feelings?

14. When a person who is not your friend, teases you, it is not teasing. It can be bullying. Explain why the difference exists.

15. What one thing about yourself you not like to be teased about – even by friends (your hair, braces, glasses, weight, height, ability to kick a ball, etc.)?**

** Use this question to have all class members make a pact to not tease each person about his/her sensitive trait. Keep this pact and support each other.

Intentional Questions: Connecting Students to a Bigger Picture

Below are some other powerful questions that connect kids to examples of bully/bystander behavior in history or broader settings and can be great tools for understanding the need for social activism.

1. Who was Hitler and why do we still talk about him today?

2. How were bystanders to blame for Hitler's rise to power?

3. If you were alive and living in Germany during Hitler's time, do you think you would have been strong enough to defend a Jewish neighbor?

4. People often make fun of what they don't know about people (race, deformity, unusual clothing, religious practices, etc.). Explain an example of this. Why do you think this happens?

5. What was 9/11 and why do we still talk about it?

6. What do you think would be the best way to change a terrorist's view of the United States?

7. What is a learning disability? We all have some learning area that we are not as strong in as others. What would it be like to work as hard as you can at a subject like math, and still not "get it"?

8. What is Attention Deficit Disorder? What is depression? What are some other health impairments that can interfere with someone's ability to learn?

9. How can having a greater understanding of a person's disabilities or health impairments help you better support a person at school?

10. All of us have some "disability" or area in which we need help. What would it take for you to feel secure enough to reach out and share the feelings and facts about your weaker areas with a peer?

An Interactive Play to Highlight the Impact of Peers Voices and Actions:
Every word, every action: makes a DIFFERENCE

How the play is used:

Tammy created the following interactive story as a tool to visually illustrate the impact judgments and comments have upon "targets" in a school setting. Once the story was completed, the students performed it for the whole school wearing multi-colored t-shirts. The "creation of the play" involved setting the school situation, inventing the characters and possible 'targeted' qualities, demonstrating how kids can be resilient, and then also how kids can seek forgiveness by making amends. The story then gets its final details from student input. We suggest you use this as a springboard for your own school wide issues, and bring in specific areas that are being targeted for bullying in your school community (specific race, gender issues, appearance, ability, etc.)

For the creation stage of this activity, the statements that the kids make to taunt as well as those said to make amends are left blank for you to fill in. Read the story to the class and let them brainstorm cruel things kids might say (ouch!). Then as the student (named Evan in the story) moves toward acceptance of his differences (and so do the other peers), classmates brainstorm comments which ask for forgiveness, serve as positive bystander behavior or make amends. (The placement of these statements are numbered, with ten different students being critical to Evan – and then the same ten, making amends.)

The story included here has adapted statements created by students. You may remove these and gather this from your own class. For example, a student makes fun of Evan for messing up when he reads aloud. "What might a mean kids say?" you can prompt. The advantage of the student input is the ownership they feel when they perform it.

To visually demonstrate the pain caused by put-downs, Tammy's school created a large red heart, which is attached to a black backdrop. Each student who made a verbal dig (as well as bystanders in some scenes, such as those who laugh or simply watch the abuse), come up and tear a piece of the heart off (we have it pre-torn and Velcro on the back so the sound is pretty powerful, too). As the narrator reads the story, the student playing Evan demonstrates the pain of having a piece of his heart torn with facial expressions and subtle body language.

When Evan makes a shift in how he responds to the comments and his own self, the students in turn begin to respond differently. As they reach out and say things to repair, they place the torn piece of his heart back. When they are done, the class can sing or present a powerful song about redemption. But visually, everyone can see that the heart, while pieced back together, has many fissures and cracks. It is important to point this out to all the students at the end of the play or in the follow-up activity included in *Making Amends*. "I'm sorry," is not the spray glue of life. It doesn't make it all better, nor erase the past. It helps targets and bullies move past a bad experience, but what works best it to think before you hurt. Every word, every action: makes a difference. Teach kids early – this is their greatest legacy. It is not your grades that you will be remembered by, nor the awards on your wall, but rather the way you treated other people. <u>It's all about relationship</u>.

A Class Play About the Impact of our Words and Actions:
Every word, every action: makes a DIFFERENCE.

Every word, every action: makes a DIFFERENCE. This is a story about the power in each of us to transform others and ourselves with our words and the words we take in, which build us up or tear us down. It is a story that reminds us we are all different. And that is okay. It is also a reminder that we have everything we need when we have faith in our ourselves and our gifts.

Evan Lee moved to a new school in the fall. His parents had divorced the year before and he now lived with his mom during the week because his dad traveled a lot.

Evan was different than other kids in the school, or at least that is how he felt. And though he knew other kid's parents were divorced, other kids were new, other kids struggled in school, other kids looked different or liked different things, he still felt more different.

He looked more like his Korean father than his Caucasian mother, and one day when his mom picked him up from carpool, a student teased him, "Did your mom buy you overseas or something?" "Were you an abandoned child, Evan?" Other kids giggled. (1) (10)

Evan used to like school. He had had a lot of friends and he was known for dribbling the soccer ball better than any other 4th grader at Sunrise Elementary School. But here, at his new school, no one knew that Evan was a good soccer player. They all seemed to like basketball better, and while Evan could dribble the ball well with his feet, his hands were not nearly as skilled, "Nice shot, Butterfingers." ridiculed another student. (2)

To top it off, he needed to wear glasses to see the board. One kid teased him when he put them on one day. "Hey four eyes!" He kept them in his desk after that. (3)

He could spell and write, but whenever he read out loud, he got nervous and always seemed to mess up the words. "Ha... maybe you should put another set of glasses on, dummy," a classmate teased and snickered. (4)

He made one good friend, Billy, but Billy had other friends too, and would often forget about Evan during recess. "Billy doesn't even like you, nerd. Go back to your old school!" one of them said. (5)

"Evan looks like a homeless street person in that coat!" he heard some kids whispering and pointing at him when he walked into school after Christmas break. His family didn't have much money, and his coat was very old and looked dirty even though they washed it often. (6)

And today, his mom's alarm didn't go off, so he raced out the door. His short black hair was sticking up in the back. "Don't you ever bother to comb your hair?" laughed a student as they lined up to go into the school. (7)

On the way into class, one of the kids tripped him and he stumbled into a coat hook. His coat ripped. Someone said, "Looks like we did you a favor – time to throw that coat away!" (8) The teacher saw and asked if he was okay. He didn't want to be a tattle-tale. He said he was fine.

One day his mom packed him Kimchee for lunch, a spicy pickled treat. "What the heck is that smelly garbage?" teased a classmate. He begged his mom to just give him a sandwich from then on. His mom smiled, "Evan, it's okay to be different. It is always okay to be yourself." (9)

But in church and when Evan prayed, Evan felt the differences melt. On the soccer field or dribbling the soccer ball in his back yard, Evan was not different. When he was with his mom or dad, or laughing with his friend Billy, Evan didn't think about his skin color, his different family, his lack of skill on the basketball court or his struggles in reading. In here, Evan felt perfect. His greatness was still inside him there – he just was forgetting and focusing on the wrong people and messages. His mom was right. His youth leader was right. His teacher was right. Evan needed to change how he responded – and also what he believed. He began to list his qualities of greatness in his head. He remembered his successes. He let go of what he couldn't do – and decided to focus on what he could.

And so Evan began to believe in himself just a bit – and the students seemed to notice, too.

Because it was good (and different!) he brought Kimchee again. He shared it with curious classmates. "Hey, sorry I made fun of you. I didn't know what it was. That stuff is actually good." (9)

Evan responded to a tease about his basketball by agreeing that he knew he wasn't very good. A student said, "You are a really good sport about us giving you a bad time. Can you teach me how to dribble the soccer ball sometime?" (2)

He laughed at himself when he stumbled over reading and a student said, "That's okay. Don't worry about it – everyone does it. You might be better at reading in your head. I know I am." (4)

He told some kids that he was going to his Dad's that weekend. Someone said, "I am sorry for saying that about your mom, Evan. I didn't really mean it. I was just trying to be cool in front of my friends."(1) "I wish I could take my words back – it was probably a difficult time for you and your parents." (10)

He squinted to see the board. A student said, "Hey, Evan. I actually thought you had really cool glasses. You should put them on. I was just teasing earlier." (3)

He got a gently-used coat from a family member as a hand-me down, and a student said, "I really love your coat, dude. Wish my mom would get me one like that." (6)

His hair was sticking up again one day. A student said, "You may not know your hair is sticking up in the back. I figured I would want someone to tell me cause mine does that all the time! " (7)

An older boy bumped him in the hall. His classmate saw him and said, "Just tell them to knock it off, Evan. It helps. I'll help you pick up your books." (8)

A group of boys invited him to play a board game during indoor recess. "Hey, Evan, you played this game with Billy yesterday. Can you play with us so we can learn it?? We really need your help." (5)

Every word, every action: makes a DIFFERENCE. This is a story about the power in each of us to transform others and ourselves with our words and the words we take in. It is a story that reminds us we are all different. And that is okay. It is also a reminder that we have everything we need when we have faith in ourselves and our gifts.

Every word, every action: makes a DIFFERENCE: Part II
Making Amends Activity Directions

This activity was created to follow-up with the play included in this chapter; however, it is powerful on its own after any story, book or class incident where students have experienced intolerance for differences. The Martin Luther King holiday, the No-Name Calling Week or Mix-it Up Day (sponsored by Teaching for Tolerance) would all be great springboards for this activity. Numerous books and movies also could be shown for connection. Begin by reading the introductory and closing paragraph if the students saw or participated in the play. Otherwise, simply ask for examples of the put-downs, the bystander behavior, the storyline and the redemption.

Lead with some powerful questions (any of the Intentional Questions in this chapter would likely be effective). Ask, "Why don't people like to be different? Is it easy to be different? Why not? Aren't we different anyway? Where does this drive come from to "fit-in"? What if we really WERE all the same? How can we be the kind of person that let's other people be different?" Kids are often quick to say it is okay to be different, so it is very powerful to point out how hard each of them work to be the same! These are healthy fodder for great class meeting discussions – and connecting the story to each person's own experience.

Next, distribute the *Making Amends* activity. Read aloud each statement slowly, pausing after each one, and ask each student to independently place a check by the statement if it is true for him or her. After the last one, ask for a simple show of hands from those who checked at least one of these statements. Flood them with their greatness by naming their courage and fearlessness to admit imperfection. "Yes, we are all great- just not perfect."

Now move them to an opportunity to make amends to someone they thought about when they checked the statements. Ideally, encourage them to name someone in their grade or class. Allow five minutes to complete the three statements. Then, ask if any further courageous person would be brave in this moment and seek forgiveness by apologizing to another student in the class (and in front of others) for something they wish they had not done. This is the most powerful part of the activity and only effective if a supportive, safe environment of honesty has been built. I guarantee hands will go up – many kids will often apologize to the same kid (a target) and many apologies will go out to friends. It will be contagious, and as the leader, you get to really honor and praise the risk-taking involved. A public apology holds the person to a higher level of character. Classmates hear and therefore can become positive bystanders if the student slips off their greatness pedestal and teases the child again. It takes a team approach to being great – and really brings a class together.

Follow this up and repeat an adapted form of it throughout the year. We always run out of time. It becomes contagious to be renewed and forgiven. While the heart is never fully repaired after a public apology, it heals with some scars (shown clearly in the play). But if the <u>actions</u> (not just the intentions) really do change, both target and offender are given a chance to be greater in all relationships in the future.

MAKING AMENDS...A Follow-Up Activity

Part I:

Place a (courageous) check mark next to each statement if the statement is true for you in the past year. Names and examples are not necessary.

_____ I have left someone out before.

_____ I have not included or invited someone to join even though I knew they wanted to.

_____ I have passed on a rumor about someone.

_____ I have run away from someone I didn't want to be with.

_____ I told someone else not to hang out with someone.

_____ I have called someone a name.

_____ I blamed someone else for something I did.

_____ I called someone a name back – after they hurt me.

_____ I probably have done other things to hurt people.

Part II:

Now I get to make amends. Every day I get to start new. But so does another person because I get to show them I am great – and getting greater every day.

I owe an apology to......

Because .....

I hope they forgive me. I plan to show them I will be different by doing/saying.....

_____   _____

Your Name   Date

SHIFTING THE ENERGY IN A PEER MEDIATOR PROGRAM FROM THE STUDENT PROBLEM TO THE STUDENT STRENGTH:
Tammy's Take on NHA and Mediation

When I began my work and real ownership of the Nurtured Heart Approach, I realized it conflicted with our somewhat effective (and Golden Apple winning) Peer Mediation Program. Taking the qualities of greatness to heart, and the need to shift from energy around the person's problem, to energy around a person's capability, I adapted how mediation works with my team of students.

Below, I outline the structure of my program (training, identifying, and coaching). Handouts and some of my forms follow. Though it is not an element of the Nurtured Heart Approach, I know many schools have these in place. Ours has been a very effective tool, particularly on our playground. And it has brought peace building to a visible place.

Selecting Mediators

When I originally began this program, I adapted the Natural Helpers system of identifying students by peer nomination. (Previously, I had been a trainer for that exceptional peer mentoring program for many years.) After the second year (and especially now as my goal is to empower individuals to their own self-confidence), I altered the selection process to one of self-nomination.

Students in grades 5-7 can complete the commitment form, get a parent signature, get two school-related adults signatures, and get four peers to sign in support of their nomination. (I do not train our 8th graders, but all students trained are mediators until graduation. The scheduling of 85 children each year is a true test of patience.)

As I only train 30 each October, I then send the list of names out to teachers for screening (i.e. Is there a student on this sheet you believe would NOT be successful as a peace-builder at this time?). Then I literally, and quite neutrally, put them into grade level and gender piles, and draw. All students who apply in 5th grade will eventually be trained. The unbiased method I use has made the: "Sorry, not this time" letters easier to handle, but always one of my least favorite steps.

Training the Mediators

Originally, we began doing a two-night training, but because of cost and time, I now do the training in a 30-hour program with just one night at a local retreat facility. The graduation ceremony is at 4 p.m. that afternoon. (Generally, I have been utilizing a teacher in-service day, so as to not take kids out of school and to have the support staff I need without requiring subs.) A myriad of resources are available out there to create your training models, and I have supplemented mine with many of these. We move from the Getting-to-Know-You activities (interspersed throughout the mini-weekend), to Understanding Human Needs for connection and belonging, to Managing and Defining Conflict, to Handling Anger, to Recognizing Point of View, to Practicing Active Listening, and then Utilizing Positive, Collaborative Resolution steps. The curricula available highlight these skills and concepts at different levels. (I list several of the publications I have accessed at the end of this section, but new materials are created yearly that match the consistent protocol.) My differentiation of these standard objectives, however, is the shift from simply energizing the problem to highlighting a disputant's capacity to handle conflict, as well as demonstrating the interdependence the parties in dispute have as they honor each other's gifts and abilities (even during the mediation).

Nurtured Heart permeates all of this: In naming our own greatness, in naming qualities and evidence of greatness in our co-mediators, in handling resets. (Even motivated kids need to be brought back to their greatness when they forget.) Additionally, the mediation steps have been adapted to move those in conflict toward greater inner wealth.

The Mediation Steps

Mediators are trained to work in pairs, to work with peers (usually no more than two at a time) in conflict and help them seek a peaceful resolution. The emphasis of this approach is to empower the students involved with the skills to work it out (skills they already possess, but fail to use when under stress).

After ground rules of mediation are laid out alternatively by the mediators (sitting across from each other) to the disputants (also sitting across from each other in a four-pointed star), the mediators ask each person to say two things that he likes about himself (things that are great, qualities that sustain them). Mediators are prompted to nudge them if stuck, by demonstrating themselves. The first disputant names the qualities and the mediators ask the second disputant to repeat what #1 has just said.

Disputant #1 (Jim): *Um... well, I am good at math. And I am a good friend.* (his voice placing the latter as a question.)

Mediator 1: *Great. Greg (Disputant 2), could you tell us what Jim just said?*

Greg: *He said he was good at math and that he was a good friend.*

Mediator 2: *Right. Okay, now Greg, tell us two great things about you?*

And so it goes. (Our Mediation Steps are included at the end of this chapter for clarification.) From this point we move into telling the story, identifying how it felt and what each disputant wants to have happen. The other disputant is prompted to paraphrase after each statement or story. The mediator must sometimes model this initially.

The perspective-taking is the core element of mediation. Listening and then paraphrasing what they hear helps teach disputants that points of view are not wrong – just different. Mediation is an intentional process which exists to slow down intense emotions long enough to diminish their negative impact, and then to provide the opportunity to hear another person's point of view. Mediators are encouraged to focus on the feelings more than the story. Feelings are never wrong. And having the person in conflict restate how a situation made the other student feel is critical to resolution. Stories can have different versions. As in the award-winning movie, *Crash,* one person's reality is just that. Their truth. Disputants can learn that the real truth of a matter is the <u>feelings</u>. Disputants get the chance to have direct experience in handling strong emotions and being able to calm themselves down enough to listen to feelings (and use WORDS to express their own feelings).

Helping students focus more on the feelings and the resolution (on their own power and the future, rather than the problem and the past) is essential in Nurtured Heart mediation. Standard mediation will have disputants take turns and share the problem, and also how it makes them feel. However, our trained mediators work more energy on the strengths of the disputants and honoring a solution (with very little time on the problem retelling). Problems do not make us stronger, but our quick ability to find solutions does.

After the brainstorming solution portion, the agreement and signing of the contract, the mediators revisit the Greatness element. This time disputants are called to name a quality of greatness in their peer, the one with whom they have just resolved the conflict. Mediators encourage the disputants to consider how their peer agreed to resolve this, stayed focused during the mediation and added ideas. They might prompt a disputant, "Greg, perhaps you can add something about how Joe communicated during today's mediation?"

At the end, mediators once again recognize the disputants for their courage, their problem-solving skills and patience. They remind them that now that they know the steps, they can likely solve similar problems on their own.

A Final Note

I am in my 8th year of this program, and have trained more than 240 students. Each year, I am amazed how many kids continue to want to become mediators, and more critically, how terrific they are at being peace-builders. No surprise to you, I am sure, that they are great role models for adults, too.

Forms/resource pages:
1. The Mediation Steps
2. Self-Nomination form
3. The Mediation Agreement
4. Brainstorming Page
5. Teaching activity for Positive Recognition Stage
6. Resource page

MEDIATION STEPS

1) Introduction Stage.

   a) Introduce mediators.
   b) Refer to disputants by name – record on Mediation Report Form.
   c) Review ground rules (take turns speaking throughout)
         i.   Disputants must agree to focus on SOLUTIONS more than the problem.
       ii.   No Name-Calling.
     iii.   Do Not Interrupt.
     iv.   Be as honest as you can
      v.   Mediation is confidential (explain if necessary.)

2) Positive Recognition/Interdependence Stage

   a) Have each disputant to share three (3) things they are great at or something positive about their personality they want you to know (Remember – you can prompt them by saying they are good at Problem Solving! That is why they are here!)
   b) Have the other disputant repeat the other's named strengths.
   c) Point out that this is called paraphrasing (or retelling for younger children). This is the skill they will use to solve their problem.

3) Help Disputants Define the Conflict: Storytelling.

   a) Ask each disputant, *"What happened, what do you want, how do you feel"*
   b) Have each disputant paraphrase/retell/restate/summarize what the other person has said for fact and feeling. Add details they leave out.
   c) Ask the original teller, *"Is that correct?"* to clarify the details.

4) Help Disputants Brainstorm solutions.

   a) Go back and forth and have disputants come up with at least 3 options.
   b) Accept all options and encourage creative thinking (you may suggest some that they had not thought about – even negative ones that would escalate the problem so they can understand their positive choice.)
   c) When all options are exhausted, have them decide which one is closest to a win-win and will keep the problem from happening again.
   d) Ask, *"Does this take care of the problem for both of you?"*

5) Agreement Writing and Positive Recognition

   a) Mediators paraphrase what each disputant has agreed upon.
   b) The agreement is written on the Mediation Report form.
   c) All sign – and form is put in the counselor's office.
   d) Ask each disputant to say something specific and positive about the other disputant before they leave. Mediators model this for them.
   e) Congratulate Mediators and Remind them of confidentiality. (If friends ask, what will you say? Prompt: The issue has been resolved.)

PEER MEDIATOR NOMINATION FORM

I am interested in being trained as one of the new 30 Peer Mediators for _____ School (grades 5-7). I am able to attend the training beginning at _____ on _____ at _____ _____ until _____ (ending around _____). Additionally, I know that after training, I will be expected to **give up at least one recess or lunch time to serve as a mediator on the playground**, after school at our after care program and/or as requested by a coordinator or teacher during school hours. Additionally, I will be expected to **attend all meetings** and **follow-up trainings**. I understand I also earn community service hours – and can take part in similar programs at the high school due to this training. I know also, that names are drawn by lottery – and my name may not be drawn for this year.

By nominating myself, I understand the role of the mediator in helping other students resolve conflicts, handling responsibility, promoting empathy and a sense of fairness, commitment to the program (until I graduate from _____), willing to strengthen my communication skills and develop more confidence in working with others. If my parents or I have questions, I can contact _____, our school counselor, by email at _____, voice mail at _____ or in person. I welcome this learning opportunity and a chance to develop the skills to be a conflict mediator at our school!

DETACH AND KEEP FOR YOUR INFORMATION – RETURN COMPLETE FORM BELOW TO: _____ **by 3:00 pm on** _____

****

PEER MEDIATION SELF-NOMINATION FORM

_____   _____   _____
My name   Class   Date

_____
My Signature

The following
        1. Students (may be a grade younger or older),
        2. School faculty, and
        3. Parent,
<u>**also**</u> **believe I could benefit the school's mission and program by participating.**

1. _____   _____   _____
    Student Signature   Class   Date

2. _____   _____   _____
    Student Signature   Class   Date

3. _____   _____   _____
    Student Signature   Class   Date

1. _____   _____   _____
    Faculty/Staff Signature   Class   Date

2. _____   _____   _____
    Faculty/Staff Signature   Class   Date

3. _____   _____   _____
    Parent Signature   Class   Date
    Daytime contact phone and email: _____

STUDENT MEDIATION REPORT

Today's Date: _____   Time mediation began: _____

Student mediators: _____ (full name and class)

                             _____ (full name and class)

Students IN mediation:

1) _____ (full name and class)

2) _____ (full name and class)

Note: If more than 2 students request mediation – select 2 to represent issues – others can mediate separately – note names of others here

_____

What is one positive quality shared about each disputant above?

     1)   _____

     2)   _____

What was the conflict generally about?

_____

_____

_____

_____

_____

(Problem Solving: Brainstorm on the back.) Was the conflict resolved? __ Yes __ No

The students have agreed that:

_____

_____

_____

SIGNATURES: _____ _____

Date: _____   Follow-up required? __ Yes __ No

(Mediators: Remember to place this completed confidential form in the coordinator's office or box.)

BRAINSTORMING ACTIVITY additional role-play

David: You embarrass me at recess because you hover around me. I like to play with you sometimes, but sometimes I like to play with other people. It feels like you are controlling me and my other friends don't like it either.

Jake: Just yesterday we played basketball together. Now you want me to find another game because you think I am bugging you. You seem to like me around sometimes and then are irritated whenever Connor or Jill are around.

What can David and Jake do to resolve their conflict so that both get what they want and like each other better than ever? Follow the 5 rules for brainstorming.

BRAINSTORMING

1. **Accept and write down all ideas without judgment or criticism.**
2. **Don't discuss any one idea until all ideas have been written down.**
3. **Both people need to add to the list. Go back and forth – try for 3 ideas each!**
4. **If the other person's idea makes you think of another, be sure to write them down.**
5. **Also try and think of ways you can handle the same situation if it happens again.**

What are the issues to be resolved?	*What are some possible solutions?*
1.	*1.*
	2.
	3.
2.	*1.*
	2.
	3.

Resources used for adapting and supporting the Peer Mediation Training and Program:

(Note: Tammy has found many things on public domains online. Additionally, she adapts many things from each resource based upon changing needs each year. These are some of the resources she has found useful in creating activities for her retreats and follow-up trainings. Every year, she adds to the resources accessed with new publications or ideas.)

Students Resolving Conflict by Richard Cohen c. 1995
 (www.schoolmediation.com)

Youth Helping Youth: A Handbook for Training Peer Facilitators by Robert Myrick and Tom Erney, c. 2004

Peer Mediation Skills: A Handbook for Peer Mediators by John DeMarco c. 1998

Conflict Resolution and Peer Mediation created by Western Regional Center for Drug-Free Schools and Communities

My Mediation Notebook by Johnson and Johnson

Kids Can Care by Joseph Six and Elizabeth Marlor, c.1996

Natural Helpers: A Peer-Helping Program developed by Comprehensive Health Education Foundation, Seattle c. 1997

The Inner Wealth Initiative: The Nurtured Heart Approach for Educators by Howard Glasser and Tom Grove, c. 2007

Activities That Teach (as well as More Activities and Still More – three different incredibly useful tools for teachers and group leaders) by Tom Jackson c. 2000

BRINGING NHA TO SPECIAL SCHOOL SETTINGS:
Group Homes and Day Treatment Centers

The upside-down ratio of relationship to problems can be extreme in group homes and day treatment centers, simply by the nature of the established structured environment. Staff members are committed to making the effort to be positive with kids. However, children in these settings, generally receive significantly more attention and energy when they are agitated or breaking rules. Kids often get restrained for simple issues of compliance (a practice which is being questioned because of the numbers of injuries and even deaths which have resulted). When a restraint occurs, a child has all the attention of the staff member physically controlling the child. These children also receive physical contact, which they may truly crave, despite its negative nature.

Louisa worked for four years in an adolescent day treatment program where the teacher and she were both too small to restrain the students. Time and time again there was a child who would be angry and threaten someone else, but the child would not actually do anything physical until one of the large, male, mental health assistants was in the room. As soon as these students knew they could "go off" and someone big enough was there to restrain them, they did. If there were no large males around, they kept it together. Louisa never once feared for her safety, because she saw the level of control the kids actually had. After the children were restrained (often requiring the energy of three or four people), and they had calmed down, they would be required to "process". Processing involved talking with the mental health assistants, the child's therapist, the teacher, the classroom therapist, etc. A whole lot of energy and excitement went into problems. Children got relatively little energy for the good choices they made.

This upside-down system is very problematic because children who make it to day treatment are <u>experts</u> at getting negative attention. It takes a lot for children to get themselves into an environment where three to four staff are present for every 12 students. For the energy-starved child it does not matter that the attention is negative: he will do whatever it takes to get more of it. For this reason, it is essential to keep all three legs of the NHA stool solid. Do not be surprised if new students are resistant and test the NHA system. Children in day treatment centers have an enormous negative self-portfolio. Start with the Camera technique and use it often. Let the children know they are seen, without putting any judgment on what you see until they start to get comfortable with the new way of doing this attention-getting business. (*Ariel, I see you taking a seat and getting your books out. Doug, your eyes are on the speaker. etc.*)

Staff, as well as students, in these settings often thrive on crisis. Employing NHA may require a real shift in roles. For example, if there is a separate time-out room, the goal should be for that staff member to set up special time with students who are doing well. If a child needs to have time away from the classroom, she gets no interaction with the staff member, other than being told where to sit. When her time is over, the staff member might tell the child she has done well doing her work and has used the time out effectively. Staff should establish when they will make time for the student if she is able to go back to class and get back on task. When students return to class, they should be welcomed warmly, with the assumption that they are starting with a clean slate.

Another obstacle to implementing NHA can be parents. These children usually come from very dysfunctional homes, so be sure to educate the parent or guardian in the core concepts of the Nurtured Heart Approach. Therapists should demonstrate this way of being in relationship during family sessions as well as during individual guardian meetings. Teach guardians to understand the power of attention, energy, consistency of rules, and the flooding of positive attention toward what is going right. Offer the trainings as a way for the parents or guardians to learn about methods to increase their children's success both at school and at home, as well as a way to better understand what their children are doing at school.

Day treatment and residential treatment centers usually have very complex Level Systems where children move up levels by demonstrating their success behaviorally. When they have a blow-out, they lose all privileges and are brought back down to the starting level. It does not matter if they have had a really good morning and then had a blow-out (say after a really difficult therapy session). All that matters is the blow-out. They go to "process" with staff about the blow-out, spend time in the quiet room or detention area, and when they have calmed down and come back to class, they are put back on the bottom level. It does not matter if they were actually pretty safe when they blew-out (not actually throwing anything at another person, just throwing stuff around) or that they did any number of other things to control themselves.

A better way to do a Level System in these settings is to use an NHA Credit System. Students earn points and spend points based on following the rules, being responsible about their work, being positive in their interactions with others, etc. Once they have earned those points, they keep those points until they spend them on privileges. At the end of each day, children should be told how many points they earned and why. Be sure to give partial credit for any incident of the type of behavior you want to increase. For example, if you get 20 points for following directions and Johnny followed directions only one time that day, give 5 points for that incident. You can say, "Johnny, when we were going out to P.E. and everyone was instructed to line up, you did that right away. That was really great following directions so I'm going to give you points for that." You don't need to say things like, "You could have earned a lot more if you would have followed directions the rest of the day."

Make it clear to the students that they might earn more points if they are able to give concrete examples of things they did right in a calm way, but that complaints about how many points they earn will not get them anywhere. Our intention is to increase a children's awareness of their behavior, so an acceptable advocacy statement might be, "Miss Louisa, I followed directions when you asked me to return to my seat at the start of group." This allows you to honor the child's self-awareness and strengths. "You're right, Johnny, that is a perfect example of following directions and advocating for yourself without complaining. I will give you more points for that!" (See credit system attached.)

If a violent incident or destruction of property occurs, using the Restorative Justice principles is very effective (see the chapter on School Discipline). With this system, children do not feed their negative portfolio of themselves. There is much more opportunity to show kids that they are doing things right. Privileges should be put on-hold until children complete their community service/Restorative Justice. Once that is done, they are free to earn points again and to spend points on privileges.

Of course, an occasional restraint may still be needed. If a child is about to attack someone else, he must be stopped. But if it is just a matter of not following a rule, ***so what***? Does it REALLY matter? The intention is to keep energy toward capability – and keep power-struggles out of the mix. <u>Broken rules should not be taken personally.</u> Give the child a reset, and all privileges should be put on hold until the reset is done. As in any setting, the reset should be

SHORT. For an emotionally-disturbed child, a three minute time-out can seem like an eternity. Ten to 30 seconds will ensure greater compliance and allow the children to come more quickly back to their greatness pedestals – and time-in.

If a child does start to destroy something, get the other children moved out of the room where they will be safe. Destroying stuff is not the end of the world. It can be fixed. The Greeks have a wonderful tradition of breaking plates at celebrations. They do this to show that their *relationships* with each other are much more important than objects. Objects can be mended or replaced. That is not the case with relationships. Once children have calmed down, help them think of some sort of community service project or Restorative Justice activity which they can do to make amends for their actions (amends with both staff and other students). This way they make their own decisions, and it is not about the staff controlling them. They are in charge of themselves. Even after making poor choices, there is always an opportunity to build a child's inner wealth.

The following is an example of a credit system that could be used in any environment. (These are adapted from Howard Glasser's first book, <u>Transforming the Difficult Child</u>.) You can keep track of points using a bank book, pretend money, or a point sheet. Add your own "Ways to Earn" and "Ways to Spend."

CREDIT SYSTEM: Ways to Earn Points

Add rules, responsibilities, and bonus points to fit each child's goals. Use pretend money, a bank deposit book or a simple point sheet to track their "banked" points for future "spending."

FOLLOWING RULES

POINTS	BEHAVIOR DEMONSTRATED
10	No Name Calling
10	No Shouting Out in Class
20	Follow Directions First Time Asked

RESPONSIBILITIES

POINTS	BEHAVIOR DEMONSTRATED
10	Staying on task
10	Bringing materials needed to class
20	Completing Class work

BONUS POINTS

POINTS	BEHAVIOR DEMONSTRATED
10	Being cooperative
10	Using free time well
20	Being supportive/helpful to a peer

CREDIT SYSTEM: Ways to Spend Points

Privileges and rewards should be listed below as they relate to the child's specific interests and the intention of your program. Examples below can be adapted for these needs.

Pts Needed	Privilege or Reward
10	Recess time
100	15 minutes one-on-one time with chosen staff member for activity (basketball, snack, etc.)
10	Healthy snack purchase
30	"Junk food" snack purchase
50	Free time on the computer (minutes = _____)
200	Field trip

BEFORE YOU CAN NURTURE OTHERS,
YOU GOTTA START WITH YOURSELF:
Recognizing Greatness

What if you went about your entire life trying to bring forth the "greatness" in every person you met? You would stop and notice. You would honor and name every great thing you saw, so enamored by their gifts and the values they exhibit.

We have always maintained a core faith that all people are good. While some may not manifest this goodness in their actions consistently, it lies within them – perhaps untapped, unrecognized even by themselves. These people have let their mirror reflect only what others have said about them, what negative beliefs they have owned about the world, themselves, and their journey. They live in their problems and their past. Yet we believe all people have the best of intentions: the <u>best</u> intention to be the best of themselves that they can. They fall short when their brain goes right to the anger/fear/worry that is often their first thought in a new situation, or one where experience has taught them to not trust. They have forgotten to be enamored with themselves.

Imagine the power they would possess, the power <u>you</u> would possess, if you were to live as though you were great, to honor your greatness always. Own it: You are great. This life is not about survival but about living, not a discovery process, but a recovery process of your ultimate greatness which has always been there.

Think now of the people who move you, those who seem to have some light which draws you and others in – those who seem to be closer to the source the way a small child is in his simplicity. Are these people actively participating in feeding their greatness? I believe so.

Wayne Dwyer, in his book *Inspiration,* cites some research done on the powerful impact of honoring people verbally. What he has learned is this: When someone hears a compliment, his or her levels of serotonin soar. This neurotransmitter is responsible for joy and satisfaction and happiness (reduced amounts of this in our brains, triggers depression). Additionally, the researchers have studied both the giver of the compliment and the witnesses and found the same results. Chemically, we are altered by the simple gift of a compliment, the recognition of our greatness.

So before we can begin to impact the souls and journeys of others, we must begin with the difficult part of ourselves. We must – we <u>must</u> – learn to accept our own greatness. FEARLESSLY accept your greatness. Often it is easy to find the beauty, depth, and shine in other people. When we aim our hearts and actions and words on others - when we shine our light on their greatness - when we name it - and are specific, we are often noticing the very qualities which we ourselves possess, but fail to shine.

Are we to create a world of arrogant braggarts who toot their own horns? Yes, I think we shall. The difference is that we don't need to defend our greatness by naming our gifts in public. When we do this, it often comes from our insecurities about ourselves: *See me prove I am worthy.* Rather, we name our Qualities of Greatness (Q.O.G.s) to ourselves - we accept them in ourselves – and in the observations of others. We acknowledge that this is hard: to see how great and powerful we are. But we know we cannot begin to impact change on the world and on the people we touch in our lives, if we are not firmly affirming our OWN greatness. Say to yourself, "*I am great.*" Then risk to name what is great about you (compassionate, brave, patient, tolerant, positive, funny, flexible, risk-taking, etc.) Keep going. Your list is endless.

Now ...

Imagine what this power, this light, this internal shine would do for a child who REALLY believes in his/her own greatness. If children or adults have this *inner wealth*, they would never harm themselves. They would think they rock, they would value themselves, and they would know their importance in the world. Imagine nurturing the soul of children so nothing could stop them in their relentless pursuit of the positives. This is a way of relating to children which focuses all your energy on their positive qualities, choices and efforts - and rewards none of their negative choices. You are in relationship with every person's best side – soaking him or her in their greatness.

"What about when I am not great?" asks the skeptical voice. Ah, that is just the old loop of negative self-bashing. It does not serve to focus on flaws. Reset. Refresh. Let it go. Bless and release. Change the default setting. For many, it can be a struggle to focus on your greatness, to stop your negative loop. Fan the flames of greatness in you and others. It's a stretch for some, but you are stretching. Negative thoughts exist, but no longer have power over you.

All this sounds so mushy and oozy and well, basically, <u>simple</u>. Our soul cries to be fed. Our spirit sings to be aligned with our soul - and our children's spirits most of all. Do not tell children who you want them to be or to become, as this implies that they are not enough as they are. "You *could* be great, EXCEPT blah, blah, blah..." <u>Something</u> is great about them in this moment. Tell them. *Here is how I see you being great... This is what I love about you... Do you see this irrefutable evidence of your greatness right now?* Don't believe it works? True transformation can occur in a ten minute conversation. Flood the person you work with. Overload your in-law. Dunk the heads of your students in the full focus of your wild appreciation of their amazing gifts. These may be things you think – but don't say, the things you tell other people but not always the individual. Let go of the worry about the things they do "wrong." Start by helping them see <u>all</u> they do right. Use no "buts" and ask for nothing in return. Do it again. And then again. Text them, email them, brag about them right in front of them.

And so you begin to change the way you relate to others, how you see them and ultimately honor them. And the transformation of the most important relationships in your life begins - because you see and live GREATNESS.

Nurtured Heart Approach Book References

Transforming the Difficult Child: The Nurtured Heart Approach, Howard Glasser & Jennifer Easley (c. 2003)

The Inner Wealth Initiative: The Nurtured Heart Approach for Educators, Tom Grove and Howard Glasser, (c.2007)

Transforming the Difficult Child Workbook: An Interactive Guide to the Nurtured Heart Approach, Howard Glasser, Joann Bowdidge, Lisa Bravo, (c. 2008)

All Children Flourishing: Igniting the Greatness of Our Children The Nurtured Heart Approach – a Parenting Paradigm for the New Millennium by Howard Glasser (c. 2008)

Transforming the Difficult Child: True Stories of Triumph Edited by Jennifer Easley and Howard Glasser (Tammy Small's story appears on 57-59)

For more information about Howard Glasser's work and other resources regarding The Nurtured Heart Approach visit Glasser's website (based in Tuscon, AZ) at www.difficultchild.com, Louisa's (based in outside of San Diego, CA) at www.nurturedheartconsulting.com, or Tammy's (based outside of Seattle, WA) at www.nurturedheart.net